For the Life of the World

Langham
GLOBAL LIBRARY

For the Life of the World

The Multiplication of Simon Peter

Johannes W. H. van der Bijl

Langham

GLOBAL LIBRARY

© 2022 Johannes W. H. van der Bijl

Published 2022 by Langham Preaching Resources
An imprint of Langham Publishing
www.langhampublishing.org

Langham Publishing and its imprints are a ministry of Langham Partnership

Langham Partnership
PO Box 296, Carlisle, Cumbria, CA3 9WZ, UK
www.langham.org

ISBNs:
978-1-83973-684-1 Print
978-1-83973-732-9 ePub
978-1-83973-733-6 Mobi
978-1-83973-734-3 PDF

British Library Cataloguing-in-Publication Data
A catalogue record for this book is available from the British Library

ISBN: 978-1-83973-684-1

Cover & Book Design: projectluz.com

For my children and my grandchildren,
physical and spiritual

Contents

Appendixes

Foreword

I met Johannes and Louise, his charming and gracious wife, in South Africa at the Society of Anglican Missionaries and Senders (SAMS-USA) retreat several years back. We had an immediate affinity. It deepened as the days went by and I became more blessed with the presence of this extraordinary couple. As the retreat ended, we parted with the awareness that, separated by thousands of miles, we might never meet again. But God had other plans.

We met again at the New Wineskins International Missionary Conference in the United States some months later. Johannes was teaching mini seminars on discipleship, and, as I sat in his classes, I became more aware of the depth of scholarship with which he presented. But even more obvious was his passion for "making disciples who can make disciples," as well as his deep love for the Lord who gave us that commandment. Over meals and conversations during breaks our friendship grew.

In the ensuing years, I have come to know a man whose driving passion is to serve his Lord and to teach others how to fulfil the Great Commission: to make disciples of all nations (Matt 28:19). In many ways, Johannes has endeavoured to do just that; as a lay missionary in Namibia, an ordained Anglican Priest serving in the United States, India, the Philippines, and in Egypt, as the founding Dean of St Frumentius Anglican Theological College in Gambela, Ethiopia, and now as an itinerant teacher and trainer working in several Southern African countries under the auspices of SAMS-USA.

With the publication of his first book, *Breakfast on the Beach: The Development of Simon Peter*, Johannes has moved on from sharing his wisdom with small groups in a few countries to reaching thousands globally, believers and unbelievers, young and old. Reading the endorsements in the front of the book, you realize the breadth of his influence on international scholars and theologians alike, and yet parents and grandparents of ten- and eleven-year-old children have written to let him know how the children's lives have been positively changed by the book. This is the nature of his skill in writing. Deceptively simple yet profoundly deep, touching all walks of life.

For the Life of the World: The Multiplication of Simon Peter, Johannes's second published work, continues Peter's story, and offers deep insights into the lives of first-generation followers of Jesus who wrestle with the application of this new and yet ancient faith, who go way beyond evangelism, making disciples who can make disciples, effectively multiplying themselves by intentionally and substantially investing in the lives of others. I believe Johannes's own storm-tossed childhood and multifaceted adult life has gifted him the ability to grasp and appreciate the challenges faced by these early believers so that he might write so compellingly and eloquently about their struggles, their sorrows, and their spirituality.

I implore you to endeavour to set aside your personal cultural biases so that you may fully enter the world of Peter and his colleagues as they seek to apply, in their own first-century world, the radical, life-changing teaching of the man they once called Rabbi, whom they now worship as their resurrected Lord and God. Join them on their joyful yet tumultuous journey of personal growth and global kingdom expansion, and you will find a new depth to your own walk of faith.

Let the adventure begin!

Rev. Dr. "Padre" Richard Copeland

The Hermitage, Texas, USA

Epiphany 2022

Preface

Disciple making is a process that does not end with the conversion of an individual. Indeed, conversion is only the beginning of a journey that ultimately leads to maturity and fruitfulness. In my previous book, *Breakfast on the Beach: The Development of Simon Peter*, I examined the method of Jesus in the growth of Simon Peter as a disciple. In this current volume, I seek to examine his further growth, post ascension, especially how he applied Jesus's method of disciple making in his own ministry – in other words, how he invested in the lives of his disciples as Jesus had invested in his.

The underlying principle of Jesus's discipleship method is one of multiplication. Invest in the lives of a few who, in their turn, each invest in the lives of a few more, who are then able to continue this method in the lives of yet more individuals. Basic multiplication rather than addition. This principle is clearly seen in Paul's comment to Timothy in 2 Timothy 2:2, "You have heard me teach things that have been confirmed by many reliable witnesses. Now teach these truths to other trustworthy people who will be able to pass them on to others" (NLT).

Peter's method is not as clear in the book of Acts as is Paul's, but that does not mean he did not apply the principle in his ministry. John Mark was certainly one of his early disciples and, from what we are able to discern from his two Epistles and the early church fathers, he must have invested in the lives of those who took up leadership positions in the churches he established in various areas outside of the borders of Israel, especially in Rome.

The fact that the early believers viewed him as a pillar of the church and that his influence in the expansion of the church throughout northern Turkey and in Rome is attested to within the lifespan of the first two generations, and the fact that the church continued to flourish after he had been martyred, shows that Peter must have raised up mature individuals who were well able to continue what he had started in Jerusalem.

I have endeavoured to faithfully follow the chronology of Peter's story recorded by Luke in the book of Acts. However, Peter disappears as a character in Acts 15 after the Jerusalem Council and we are not told, in Scripture, exactly where he went to. For this part of his life, I relied on statements made by Paul in his Epistles, statements made by Peter himself in his Epistles, statements made by the early church fathers, and on a few ancient traditions. Some stories are purely speculative, and I have employed quite a bit of literary licence in places. For this reason, the latter part of the book is not quite as detailed as the former.

As with my previous volume, my intention is to demonstrate the method of Jesus in and through the life of the apostle Peter. It is my hope and prayer that the readers of both volumes will be encouraged and exhorted to continue to use this effective system for the expansion of our Lord's kingdom.

Johannes van der Bijl

De Kuilenaar,

Heiloo, The Netherlands

Acknowledgements

In many ways, this book has been like a rather demanding cross-country marathon, passing through pretty meadows and woodlands, but also taking me up some challenging mountain passes and along steep cliff edges. But I have not been alone in this race. As always, I have always had my teammate, Louise, by my side as well as also those who cheered me on along the way, especially when treading the unfamiliar territory of church tradition. And, of course, there are those who kept reminding me of the need for a sequel to *Breakfast on the Beach*. I am truly grateful for the love and the support and for the trust . . . and for all the egging on!

I also wish to thank our sending agency, SAMS-USA, those at Trinity School for Ministry, especially librarian Susanah Hanson, and the other kind folks who made it possible for me to sit in the library for many hours (and to use their internet service!), as well as those fortitudinous folks at Langham Publishing who put up with me throughout the process, especially Mark Arnold, Luke Lewis, and Joel Slater.

And then I also wish to thank Peter Leithart for his help via email when I felt out of my depth with some of the more difficult parts of 1 and 2 Peter.

But ultimately, all my thanks goes to my eternally patient and gracious Lord for all his goodness in giving me such a wonderful host of enthusiastic co-labourers in the kingdom.

Preamble

It was a crowded hole . . . too small to accommodate all its wretched occupants comfortably. Yet, in spite of their natural body heat, and their being pressed together, flesh against flesh, it was cold, dark, and wet. Mould grew prolifically on the walls, olive green in colour, elsewhere black and foul smelling. The prison stank of sweat, of rotting food, and of the faeces and urine of countless prisoners over the years . . . a stench so terrible it could hardly be endured.

Peter had been imprisoned before, in the Antonio Fortress in Jerusalem, but nothing could have prepared him for the horror he entered when they threw him down through the hole into this subterranean chamber. He had no idea where his dear wife, Perpetua,[1] and Petronilla, their daughter,[2] were at that time. Were they warm and safe? . . . or cold, hungry, and fearful? He prayed that they were in a better place, and that they were being treated with a measure of respect. Some called this dungeon the portal to hell – in times past, people had worshipped demons at the spring that gushed out of the floor. Peter thought back to a happier time when Jesus had taken them to Caesarea Philippi. The spring there was also said to be a portal to hell where people offered goats, or sometimes even their children, to the Greek god Pan. But that was a beautiful place . . . this prison *was* hell.

Thankfully, Peter's incarceration here was temporary . . . another fate was waiting for him . . . one that Jesus had told him about many years before as they shared that wonderful breakfast on the beach in Galilee. Jesus had also told him earlier that the very portals of hell would not be able to withstand the steady advance of the gospel. So he took every opportunity, with no thought as to how long he might still have to live on earth, to introduce his fellow prisoners to the Lord he loved so dearly. Some believed, and Peter baptized them in the water of the spring that had once served a very different purpose. There in the filth and in the stench, he told them stories about Jesus . . . about the light that could overcome darkness, about an inheritance in a kingdom that even death itself could not steal away from them. At times, he painted such vivid pictures in his stories that, in their imaginations, they were transported to the plains

---

1. There is no biblical or extra-biblical evidence for this name. I have named her Perpetua for the sake of the narrative.

2. *The Roman Martyrology*, (4th century) names Petronilla as Simon Peter's daughter.

where Jesus fed five thousand people with five loaves and two fishes, to the heights of Mount Hermon, to the depths of the Jordan valley. They plunged into the waves of the stormy Sea of Galilee . . . they backed away in terror from the Gadarene demoniacs . . . they wept and rejoiced with the widow of Nain and with Jairus and blind Bartimaeus. He told them of that awful dark night when he denied knowing his Lord . . . he told them of his gracious reinstatement and how that had utterly changed the course of his life.

There in the grimy, murky depths of hell itself, Peter shone out the light of the world, he plundered the strongman's household, snatching the brands out of the flames before they were lost forever, and God commanded the angels to rejoice for every lost lamb that was added to the fold. Fear was conquered by love . . . hope was ignited . . . and faith set the captives free.

This was why he was here. This was why he yet lived. The promise was not for him alone . . . the promise was not only for their children . . . the promise was for the world.

* * *

Part One

"I will breathe my Spirit into you, and you shall live again"

Ezekiel 37:14

1

Tying up Loose Ends

So, Jesus told you to keep this to yourself until after he was raised from the dead?" Andrew asked.

"Yes," Peter replied. "At first, I was worried. I wondered how I could keep a secret from you . . . as you know I've never done that before. But then the incident with the young, demon-possessed boy . . . well, I think that was a major distraction, and you never asked what happened to us while we were on the mountain."

"It was not intended to exclude you," James explained.

"Or hurt you," John added.

"But why?" Andrew asked, "Why would Jesus keep something like that from the rest of us, and only share it with you three?"

"Perhaps he felt we would not be able to describe what really happened," Peter offered. "And, in truth, we would not have been able, as you well know. What did we understand about his 'Exodus' in Jerusalem, as they called it?"

"By 'they' you mean Moses and Elijah," Andrew clarified.

"Yes. But besides that, if truth be told, none of us understood what Jesus was trying to tell us when he spoke about his betrayal, arrest, abuse, and execution . . . and even less, his talk about rising from the dead. If we had shared with you what had happened on the mountain, we would have got it all wrong."

"Your brother wanted to build three shelters for them on the mountain," James said in an attempt to lighten the awkward mood.

"What?" Andrew asked, "Why?"

"Well . . ." Peter blushed as he remembered the event, "well, what happened was . . . I feel so stupid even repeating this. I was thinking about the Psalm that speaks about God keeping us safe in a shelter, hiding us, as it were, in a shelter. So, I thought that if we could detain Jesus . . . and Moses and Elijah . . . if we could keep Jesus safe in a shelter, there on the mountain, then he would not die as he had been saying. It was my foolish attempt to protect him, that's all."

3

"No. Not foolish," John said. "You loved him, and you wanted to keep him from harm. That is not foolish, that is commendable. There's nothing stupid about that. Besides, none of us understood what he was talking about . . . none of us could have predicted what transpired on that awful cross that day. Even as I stood watching, even as he quoted from the Psalms, trying to help us understand that God had not forsaken us . . . I did not understand. All I could see was the one I loved dearly – the one who loved *me* dearly – slowly, painfully, slipping away from us. And I thought when he said, 'It is finished' . . . I thought that it was . . . I thought that it was all finished. All our messianic dreams . . . all our ambitions . . . all our hopes. What did I know of the new creation? I did not know that by saying that, he was indicating that he had completed his work of redemption . . . of restoration. To be honest, I'm still trying to get my mind around it all. It was not even close to what we were led to believe would happen."

"You know, it was only after he rose from the dead that I realized what that meant," James said. "That just as God finished his creative work and then rested on the Sabbath, so Jesus too finished his work and rested on the Sabbath."

Andrew was quiet for a moment, trying to process everything he had just heard. Then he said, "I know why he did not want you to tell us. He knew that we were going through a crisis of faith at the foot of that mountain. To add such a riddle, such a mystery to the mix, our minds were already reeling from our failure to drive out that demon. If you had told us about what had happened that night up on the mountain, we would have . . . I would have not been able to . . . well, it would have been too much."

"So much of what we know now would have been too much . . . *was* too much," Peter said. "Remember when he told us that he still had a lot more to teach us, but that we were not able to bear it at that moment? He knew we did not have the right framework . . . there were so many things, so many incorrect thought patterns to dismantle before we could insert anything new. Like that riddle he once taught us, new wine into new wineskins. Can you remember?"

"Yes, he said you could not sew a new patch on an old garment," James said, "because the patch would tear away from the old fabric, and the whole thing would have to be discarded. The same with pouring new wine into old wineskins . . . the old wineskins would burst as the new wine fermented."

"Actually, I still don't really get that," John said.

"Precisely what we have been talking about," Andrew said. "He could not pour new information into our old ways of understanding spiritual things . . . what we had been taught had to be replaced with a new framework, as Peter said."

"You know, I really think we need to start collecting his sayings – his teachings and his stories," Peter said. "We need to make sure we write this all down . . . we won't be around forever."

"Indeed!" Andrew agreed, "Are we not the people of the Book? Just like the Psalmist reminds us, God commanded our people to teach the generations to come, so that they would remember and not be like their forebears.[1] Moses and the prophets wrote what God spoke . . . we should do the same. We need to write down what Jesus taught us so that those who come after us will know what we know."

* * *

They were all gathered together in the upper room of Mary's compound. The number of believers had increased to one hundred and twenty by this time – including Jesus's brothers who had once mocked him. The one brother, by the name of James, now described himself as a slave of God and of the Lord Jesus Christ,[2] and had become a humble leader in their small community. Daily they came together to pray, as they waited for the gift Jesus had spoken about shortly before he went back to the Father in heaven.

Peter addressed the whole group one day, "My beloved brothers and sisters. I think you will all agree when I say that our number as apostles is incomplete. Jesus had intended for there to be twelve of us and, well, you all know what happened to Judas."

"I still can't believe it," Matthew said. "He was so adamant that no one would betray Jesus."

"Yes. He was," Peter agreed. "Then again, I said I would not deny Jesus . . . but I did, didn't I?"

"True," Mary of Magdala said, "but you were sorry for it . . . you repented and were restored. Judas may have regretted his decision, but remorse and repentance are just not the same thing."

"Guilt is a terribly powerful emotion . . ." Peter said, "but his action has now led to the creation of a burial ground for strangers. Something good has come out of something bad." Peter paused momentarily, "Nevertheless, the Psalmist tells us that another ought to take his place and so we need to choose someone who was with Jesus from the beginning . . . an eyewitness to his life and ministry, starting with John the Baptizer, all the way through to his resurrection."

---

1. Psalm 78:5–8.
2. James 1:1.

"Well, at least two of our brethren fit that description," Philip called out from the back.

"And they are?" Peter enquired.

"Joseph, whom we call Barsabas," Philip replied.

"And Matthias," James added.

"Anyone else?" Peter asked. After a period of silence he said, "I take it your silence means you are satisfied with these two candidates?"

Everyone nodded. Barsabas and Matthias were both godly, humble men and had already proved themselves to be faithful to Jesus and the kingdom. At the time when so many others left Jesus because his teaching was hard to understand,[3] they persevered and remained loyal to him.

"Then we need to pray for the Lord to guide us in the casting of lots," Peter said. "That's the way they allotted land in the time of Joshua[4] and also the way they decided between eligible men for offices and functions in the temple duties[5] . . . so I believe that that will be the way for us to determine the Lord's will in this matter . . . yes?"

Again everyone nodded in agreement. Andrew couldn't help thinking that all the believers had accepted Peter's leadership without question. Hadn't Jesus said he needed to care for them as his community?

"Sovereign Lord," Peter prayed, "you alone know the hearts of all. You sought the Father's guidance in the choosing of the twelve . . . one of whom proved to be a devil, as you well knew, and he has done what you said he would do. Please, guide us now in the choice of his replacement as we cast these lots."[6]

He threw the lots down on the ground. The eleven stood around them.

"Matthias!" James said.

Barsabas turned and hugged his friend. "I am glad you are the one chosen," he said. "I am not sure that this would have been a good fit for me."

"Thank you, Barsabas," Matthias replied, leaning into the hug, "I am not sure I am worthy."

"None of us are worthy," Peter said, overhearing the conversation. "This is one of the first lessons we all need to learn as followers of Jesus. We are not worthy . . . and we cannot live as we ought to live. I thought I could and I failed . . . I failed at one of the most crucial junctures of my life. And it was in my failure that I learned that I need him . . . if I am to walk as he walked, live as he lived, love as he loved . . . I need him every step of the way."

---

3. John 6:66.

4. Joshua 18:10.

5. 1 Chronicles 24:5; Nehemiah 10:34.

6. Proverbs 16:33.

"But, Peter," Matthias interrupted, "How can we do that? I mean, how do we walk *with* him? I know Jesus said he was with us always . . . even to the end of the age . . . but . . ." Matthias glanced nervously at the others, concerned that they would think him slow to learn, "but he is not here with us now . . . not really."

"That is what we are waiting for," Peter replied.

"Waiting for?" Barsabas echoed. Matthias breathed a sigh of relief, at least he wasn't the only one who did not seem to understand.

"Yes, remember he said that we must wait here in Jerusalem until he sends the promise of the Father[7] . . . the helper . . . the one who is like him[8] . . . the one who will lead us in truth.[9] The Holy Spirit. That was the promise he gave us, that he will not leave us as orphans,[10] but that he would come to us . . . that he would be with us . . . in us."

"And so we wait . . ." Matthias said.

"And so we wait," Peter confirmed.

* * *

The disciples were basking in the warmth of the sun in the courtyard of Mary's compound. Each one lost in their own thoughts. So much had happened since their world seemed to have fallen apart with the execution of Jesus . . . how little they understood then . . . how little they understood now. It had been a few days since Jesus had returned to the Father, and they were still puzzling over some of the things he had taught them in the three years they walked with him. And then there was this waiting . . . waiting for what exactly? Who was the Holy Spirit? How would his coming change anything?

John turned to Peter and broke the silence, "I thought Jesus already gave us the Holy Spirit. Remember that night when he first appeared to us all, he breathed on us and said, 'receive the Holy Spirit.'[11] You do remember that don't you? I know you were still dealing with a lot of personal shame at the time, but you did not miss that, did you?"

"No, I did not miss that. I remember it," Peter replied, "I remember it well. At the time, when he breathed over us, I thought that he was doing to us what God had done to Adam at creation. Breathing new life into us because, as descendants of Adam, we were all born in iniquity and as such we too were

---

7. Luke 24:49.

8. John 14:16.

9. John 16:13.

10. John 14:18.

11. John 20:22.

dead . . . as dead as if we had eaten the fruit ourselves . . . dead in our trespasses and sins. But since Jesus had defeated sin and death – and Satan, for that matter – he could give us life in him. I'm not sure I was right back then . . ."

"I think you were right," Matthew said. "How I see it, before his resurrection, we were as lifeless as the dirt out of which God made Adam. Dead. But somehow, through Jesus's resurrection, we were also raised to life . . . but only in him."

"In other words, those who are not in him," Andrew interrupted, "remain dead."[12]

"Exactly," Matthew replied. "Those who are not in Jesus, remain in Adam . . . or, to use Jesus's own words, only the branches that stay connected to the True Vine, can bear much fruit."[13]

"So . . . let me see if I am understanding you all correctly," Philip said. "What Jesus breathed on us was life . . . the same Spirit that raised him from the dead, now raised us to life in him. Am I right?"

"That's what I believe," Peter said.

"In that case . . . what exactly are we waiting for now?"

"Well, I've been praying about that," Andrew said. "There are three passages from the prophets that come to mind. The first is a prophecy from the scroll of Jeremiah. It really is an interesting passage . . . through the prophet, God promises that one day he would write the law – the external law written on tablets of stone and on parchments and on vellum scrolls – he would write that law on the hearts of his people, so that we might know him from within . . . and this is set in the context of God saying that he will forgive our sins and not remember them anymore."[14]

"I'm not sure I follow your reasoning," Philip interjected. "What has that got to do with what, or who, we are waiting for?"

"Well, that is where the second prophecy comes in, this time from Ezekiel. In that prophecy, God promises to not only cleanse us from our sin, but to give us a new heart and a new spirit . . . that he will remove from us the hard, deceitful,[15] stony heart, and give us a truly human heart . . . the heart we ought to have had, had our forebears not sinned. But then God went on to say that he would put his Spirit within us. So, once again, God is placing what has up until now been external, like the law, inside us. And according to this prophecy,

---

12. John 3:36; Mark 16:16; 1 John 5:12.
13. John 15:1–8.
14. Jeremiah 31.
15. Jeremiah 17:9.

it is the presence of God's Spirit that will enable us to be obedient to him.[16] God wants us to be obedient. In this we are to have the mind of Jesus, in spite of the fact that he knew obedience would lead him to the cross. But we know from history, and from our own personal experience, that we are not able to be obedient to his law. That's why we need the Holy Spirit. To help us keep the law God has written on our hearts."

Matthew shook his head in amazement, "What are you, Andrew? A walking set of scrolls? How do you remember all of that?"

Matthew's attempt to lighten the moment was lost on Philip. He was trying hard to understand. "So, what you are saying is that we are waiting for God to fill us with his Spirit . . . and his law?"

"His Spirit who will help us internalize, understand, and obey the law, yes," Andrew said. "At least, this is how I understand it. Because of Jesus's triumph over sin and death, we are alive in him . . . born again, to use his own terminology, that is why he breathed the Holy Spirit on us . . . but now . . . now, we need his Spirit to help us live according to God's law . . . to live as we ought to have lived . . . as we were created to live."

"I've been thinking a lot about this too," John interjected. "I understand the death and resurrection of Jesus in terms of the Exodus and our festivals. He is our Passover Lamb . . . he is the prophet like Moses that leads us out of slavery . . . in this case, slavery to sin. He is the first fruits of our release . . . because he lives, we live. And soon it will be the Feast of Weeks, Pentecost, in which we celebrate a good harvest and anticipate another or, if God is willing, an even greater one in the future. A time when we usually renew our pledge to uphold our part of the covenant . . . to be obedient to his law.[17] Somehow, the Spirit of God will enable us to be fully obedient and to do the same things Jesus did . . . or, as he said, even greater things than he did because he was only one, while we are many. So, in my understanding, if the same Spirit, who did the works through Jesus, lives in us, we will do more than Jesus did."

"You all are hurting my head," Thomas chimed in from where he was seated with his eyes closed. "Can't we just enjoy the sunshine in silence for a while, please?"

"You are right, John," Peter said, ignoring Thomas, "if you all remember that night when Jesus took us through the Scriptures to show us how everything

---

16. Ezekiel 36.

17. Leviticus 23:15–22. According to Jewish tradition, the law was given to Moses on Mount Sinai during the Feast of Weeks, therefore they reenact the giving of the law by reciting the Ten Commandments and renewing their vows to be obedient to the law of the covenant.

that was written from Moses through to the Prophets . . . how everything spoke of him . . . everything pointed to him. The stories, the laws, the rituals, all of those things were pictures of what he came to do."

"Wait, wait, please. Excuse me for interrupting, dear brethren, but Andrew has not finished . . . he has yet to tell us of the third prophecy," Philip reminded them.

"I apologize . . . I took you down a different trail with the Exodus," John said.

"Not at all," Andrew said, "I think that you paint a vivid portrait of what Jesus did for us on the cross. Jesus is, in many ways the completion of the story that began in the garden of Eden . . . as well as the end of the story that started with Abraham . . . and the conclusion of a greater Exodus." He paused, as if to collect his thoughts, and then continued, "But the last prophecy I was thinking about comes from the scroll of Joel. There, too, God promised to pour out his Spirit on us all – our sons, our daughters, our old men, our young men, both men and women . . . all his servants. That prophecy is also set in the context of salvation and deliverance[18] . . . and what Joel says will happen is, in many ways, an answer to Moses's prayer . . . that all God's people would be filled with God's Spirit."[19]

"But there's also judgement, surely," Philip said. "At least that's what I remember of Joel."

"Exactly! But judgement tempered by hope. There is always hope with God because there is always mercy. Remember Habakkuk? 'Temper your anger with compassion,' the prophet prayed.[20] If only his people would repent of their sins and turn back to him! But remember, Jesus said that judgement would fall on his wayward people because they refused to receive him . . . even on this generation . . . he told us that Jerusalem would be destroyed . . . that not one stone of the temple would remain standing on another," Andrew replied.

"I recall him saying, at that awful travesty of a trial, that the very ones who wrongfully judged him would see him seated at the right hand of God and coming on the clouds of heaven . . . both images of judgement from the scroll of Daniel,"[21] John said.

"But what of the temple?" Philip asked, "What about Jerusalem? If everything is to be destroyed, where's the hope in that?"

---

18. Joel 2.
19. Numbers 11:29.
20. Habakkuk 3:2.
21. Daniel 7.

"The hope lies with us . . . or more pointedly, within us . . . we believers are being built up as his temple!" Peter exclaimed. "Jesus is the cornerstone of a new temple and a new Jerusalem . . . but not a physical one built with stones. No, we who live in him, we are being built up to be a living temple in the world. Just like the prophecies indicated . . . nothing will be external anymore."

"Do you remember what Jesus said to the Samaritan woman?" John asked, adding on to Peter's train of thought.

"That a day would come when we no longer worship God in Jerusalem or any other physical location?" Andrew enquired.

"Yes . . . he said that the Father wants to be worshipped in spirit and in truth."[22]

"So . . . we are waiting for the Spirit of God to fall upon us as he did on the Tabernacle and on the temple in days gone by . . . is that right?" Philip asked, trying to piece together all he had heard them say. "*We* are the new temple? *We* are the new Jerusalem? Why is this so difficult?" he added, as if to himself. Perhaps there were too many images and explanations. It was just too much for him to take in at one time. If only he had learned the Scriptures as well as Andrew had, if only he had memorized the Scriptures as well as Andrew had . . . Andrew had truly hidden the Scriptures in his heart.[23]

"If we are to be the community of Jesus on earth," John said, "we *need* to be filled with his Spirit. Just as the Spirit was the agent of the creation, so he must now be the agent of the new creation. Remember, it was through the Holy Spirit that Jesus was conceived in the first place. Isn't that right, Mary?"

The women had been shelling field peas while the men talked, Mary pondering what was said in her heart as she was inclined to do.[24]

"That is true, yes." Mary paused for a moment, then she added, "You know, I've been listening to you all as you have been speaking. You have taken me back in time . . . the things you are discussing now, are things I have been contemplating ever since the angel Gabriel told me I would conceive through the Holy Spirit. My son . . . my Lord . . . was conceived in much the same way as Adam . . . he had no earthly father, and, as such, I believe he is the beginning of a new age . . . a new creation, if you will."

"That's right!" John exclaimed, jumping to his feet, suddenly so excited as the glorious consequences of the incarnation began to take shape in their hearts and minds. "So, too, we, as his new creatures . . . as his children . . . as

22. John 4:24.
23. Psalm 119:11.
24. Luke 2:19.

subjects of his kingdom . . . we will be born of the Spirit not of the flesh, nor of the will of man, nor of blood lineage."[25]

"But there is more—" Peter started to say.

"No! No more, please!" Philip cried, "I'm struggling to keep up with all of this as it is . . . it's getting jumbled in my brain."

"Well, let me just say this, and we can leave the discussion at that," Peter said, laughing. "Jesus said we must wait here for the outpouring of his Holy Spirit, before we do anything . . . before we witness to others about all he said and did. Because it is the Holy Spirit who will help us understand, and who will help us to recall everything . . . everything we have learned."

"In other words, he who inspired the authors of the Holy Scriptures, will now illuminate our hearts and minds to understand and apply the Scriptures to our lives," Andrew added. "And through him working in us and through us – as well as in the hearts and minds of those we encounter along the way – we will announce the good news to the world."

"We will be his light shining in the darkness," John said.

"We will be the city set on the mountain, the city that cannot be hidden,[26] the city that is not made by human hands[27] . . . a spiritual city in which Jesus is king,"[28] Peter offered.

Silence descended on the compound for a short while as each follower of Jesus was lost in their own thoughts once more. There was a sense of wonder and of anticipated excitement in the air.

Philip broke the silence, "I wonder what it will feel like. I mean, what will it be like when the Spirit of God lives within us? Will we be like Moses, or like one of the prophets . . . like Elijah or Elisha? Humble and wise, or bold and fearless? And if, as Andrew says, the law is within us, written on our hearts, will we never do anything wrong again? Will we know all there is to know? Will we be perfect?"

"I'm not sure, but I somehow doubt that last bit," Peter chuckled. "We will just have to wait and see." Turning to Andrew he said, "Joel, hey? You need to tell me more."

* * *

25. John 1:13.
26. Matthew 5:14.
27. Acts 7:48.
28. 1 Peter 2:4–8.

2

The Promise and the Power

It was the day of the Feast of Weeks . . . Pentecost as the Jews of the dispersion[1] called it, meaning fifty days. Many Jews and God-fearers from all over the world came to the festivals because the festivals gave the individual worshippers a sense of purpose and meaning, anchoring them firmly in the living story of their people. There was a vivid feeling of expectation, beginning with the purification rituals on the southern side of the temple structure. Compared with other contemporary sacred spaces, the temple was huge and impressive. Herod's use of modern Roman techniques of vaulting helped him create a massive platform on the slopes of Mount Moriah.[2] The temple itself sparkled in the sunlight as it was lavishly decorated with various golden objects of art and with enormous tapestries portraying scenes of the heavenlies.

All the followers of Jesus were gathered in the upper room of Mary's house for the prayers. The noise of the slaughtering of sacrificial animals drifted up from the temple area.[3] Suddenly, there was a deafening sound . . . like a violent wind before an approaching thunderstorm.[4]

"What is happening?" Perpetua shouted in Peter's ear.

"I don't know . . . I don't see a wind outside, I don't feel a wind . . . but I hear it," he replied.

"I think God is coming!" she shouted back. "It is like I imagine it was on Mount Sinai . . . only . . . only I am not afraid!"[5]

---

1. *Encyclopedia Britannica Online*, s.v., "Diaspora Judaism," https://www.britannica.com/topic/Diaspora-Judaism.

2. Day, *Temple and Worship*, 460. See also 2 Chronicles 3:1.

3. Leviticus 23:15–22.

4. It may be that this event is meant to recall the theophany account on Mount Sinai. Exodus 19:20.

5. Exodus 20:18–21.

"Look!" Andrew cried out.

Something that looked like flames of fire was descending on each person in the room.[6]

"What is this?" Perpetua cried out.

"God is covering us as he once covered the tabernacle and the temple!"[7] Peter shouted back. "God is taking up residence with in us. We are, every one of us, his holy temple!"[8]

"God is bestowing on us the same Spirit that once resided in Moses!"[9] Andrew yelled out. "This is an answer to Moses's prayer: 'If only all the people were prophets, filled with God's Spirit!' But more! There's more! Just like God took a portion of his Spirit from Moses and placed him on the chosen ones, so God has taken the same Spirit from Jesus, who is the prophet like Moses,[10] and is giving him to us!"

John jumped up suddenly and ran out of the compound into the streets of Jerusalem. He was talking loudly about what God had done through Jesus. Mary of Magdala followed, also speaking loudly – something that was quite out of character for her. And then Peter felt it too . . . a warmth . . . a heat . . . then a compelling urge to go out and tell people about Jesus. He looked at the others, all of them were now moving out of the compound into the city, loudly proclaiming the wonders of God. But the strangest thing of all was that not everyone was speaking in Aramaic . . . some of the words Peter heard them speak, he did not understand.

The bewildered visitors to Jerusalem as well as the residents of the city had rushed to the place from where they had heard the loud sound, only to be confounded by the hundred and twenty followers of Jesus streaming out of the compound and meeting them in the streets. There were people from many different parts of the Roman Empire, from North Africa to Asia to Gaul. What was most alarming to these pilgrims was that, although they could distinguish the speakers as Galileans because of their distinct accent, they heard them speaking in their own native tongues.[11] The group gathered more curious onlookers as they made their way to the entrance of the temple.

---

6. See Psalm 29:7 "The voice of the LORD bursts forth like flames of fire."

7. Exodus 19:16–20; 40:34–36; Numbers 9:15–23; 1 Kings 8:10.

8. 1 Peter 2:5; Ephesians 2:21–22.

9. Numbers 11:16–17.

10. Deuteronomy 18:15–19.

11. Some scholars believe that this event is portrayed as a reversal of the curse of Babel. Many Jews in the Diaspora possibly adopted the languages of their countries of domicile. See Immanuel, *Acts of the Apostles*, 25–26.

Many were assembled in that area because of the large meeting space around the ritual baths at the foot of the great steps. They began to question among themselves what was happening. Some were mocking the disciples, saying that they were drunk.

Peter was experiencing something he had never felt before . . . an inner impulse to address the crowd. It was like a warmth rising within him, calming the waves of doubt and fear, filling him with bravery. He had never done anything quite like this before; just a few weeks ago, he had been so afraid of being associated with Jesus, he had denied him, not once, but three times. Now, all he wanted to do was tell everyone about him . . . regardless of the consequences. He had to tell them what he knew to be true.

He climbed the steps to the place where Jesus had stood on the Feast of Tabernacles . . . when he had cried out that if anyone was thirsty, they ought to come to him and drink, as he was the one out of whom rivers of living waters would flow.[12] In one sense, Peter felt like he was being filled with that river[13] . . . filled to overflowing and that if he did not open his mouth to speak he would burst.[14] He motioned with his hands for the crowd to quiet down.

"Brethren," he began, "I hear some saying they think we are drunk. But it is still far too early in the morning for us to have been drinking!"

Some in the crowd laughed out loud, but others were still quite troubled by what they had just witnessed.

"What you have just observed was prophesied by the prophet Joel . . . many years ago."

Andrew looked up at his brother and smiled. They had talked about the prophecies of Joel for hours the night before. Peter was not as unlearned as some thought he was . . . as even he, himself, thought he was. So many misjudged him by his appearance, they assumed he was just an ordinary, simple, and unschooled fisherman . . . but he had learned so much in his few years following Jesus, especially since the resurrection.

"In these last days," Peter recited from memory,[15] "God said: 'I will pour out my Spirit on all people. Your sons and your daughters will prophecy. Your old men will dream dreams. Your young men will see visions. I will even pour

---

12. John 7:38.

13. Compare Ezekiel 47:1–12, John 7:37–39, and Revelation 22:1–5.

14. Cf. Jeremiah 20:9.

15. I personally witnessed the amazing ability of some to memorize large portions of Scripture when working with oral learners in Gambela, Ethiopia. A group of young Nuer children had seen the Jesus film only three times prior to our reshowing it for the fourth time one evening. As they watched, I heard them talking, but they were not repeating the words of the actors . . .

out my Spirit on the disadvantaged among you, both men and women in those days. There will be signs in the heavens and on the earth . . . blood, fire, pillars of smoke . . . the sun will fail to give its light . . . the moon will be blood red . . . before the great and awe-inspiring day of the Lord. For it will come to pass that all who call on the name of the Lord will be saved.'"

Many in the crowd began to murmur rowdily . . . they all believed that the prophecy about the day of the Lord was referring to the advent of the messiah.

"Listen to me, please!" Peter shouted above the noise of the crowd. The people quieted down once more. "You all know about Jesus, the Nazarene, the man sent from God . . . most of you witnessed his miraculous works, which God performed among you. Signs and powerful deeds and wonders . . . all affirming his authenticity. By the predetermined council and foreknowledge of God, this man was sent to you . . . but instead of receiving him, you had him executed in bold defiance of what the law requires. But . . ." Peter paused. He wanted to emphasize the way God had taken their evil deeds and used them to bring about the fulfilment of the promise made long ago to their forebears, that one day, the seed of the woman would reverse the curse.[16] "But what you meant for evil, God used for good.[17] You know death is the result of sin, but Jesus was without sin, therefore death could not hold him, and so God raised him from the dead."

Some of the disciples were moving among the crowd, explaining what Peter was saying to those who did not understand, just like the Levites did during the time of Ezra.[18] Some who had been present at the time of the crucifixion of Jesus were beating their chests as they remembered what had been done. How the multitude had cried out for the death of Jesus, while Pilate, a pagan and an evil man, repeatedly pronounced him guiltless.

"As King David once said," Peter continued, "'I have set the Lord before me . . . and so, because he is at my right hand, I will never be shaken. For this reason, I am filled with overwhelming joy, because I rest in the assured hope that God will not abandon me to the collective place of the dead . . . he will not allow his holy one to experience decay. No, he will reveal to me the way of life, and cause me to delight in his presence.' Now, think about this," Peter paused once more. The people waited in a suspense-filled silence. "Where is the

---

they were speaking with them. These youngsters had memorized the entire Gospel of Luke in three sittings.

16. Genesis 3:15.

17. See Genesis 50:20.

18. Nehemiah 8:7–9.

patriarch David now?" He paused again, giving them time to consider his line of reasoning. Everyone knew the answer to this very simple question, but Peter wanted to contrast the perceptible with the imperceptible. Some in the crowd began to point in the direction of where David's tomb was located. "Where is our great King David now? He died and was buried, right? Anyone can go and visit his tomb at any time. But David was not just a king, he was also a prophet . . . and he knew God had promised to raise up one of his descendants to occupy his throne forever. And so, foreseeing the future, he predicted that, unlike him, the messiah would not experience decay in the grave. God has fulfilled this prophecy, in plain view, by raising Jesus, a descendant of David, from the dead. We are all eye-witnesses to this reality. Now, Jesus has been exalted to the right hand of God and, having received the promise of the Holy Spirit from the Father, he has poured out on us what you now see and hear."

The people began to murmur among themselves once more. A fear had fallen on them. What had they done? Had the insane mob mentality caused them to kill their messiah . . . their only hope?

"Listen!" Peter shouted once more. "Listen to me! Quiet down! You all know well enough that David never ascended into the heavens. And yet he says, 'The LORD said to my Lord, sit at my right hand until I place all your enemies under your feet.'[19] So be assured of this fact today. This Jesus – yes, the same Jesus you crucified – God has made this Jesus both Lord and Christ."

Some in the crowd were weeping and beating their chests. Others cried out, "Tell us . . . please tell us what we must do!"

Peter shouted out, "Every one of you must repent . . . every one of you must express sincere regret for your sins . . . every one of you must turn away from your old ways . . . and be baptized into the name of Jesus Christ as a sign of the washing away . . . a burying of your past life and of your rising into a new life. And then, you too will be filled with the Holy Spirit as Joel predicted. This promise is not just for us! It is for our children . . . it is for everyone, even those who live at the ends of the world . . . as many as the Lord our God may call."

Peter continued to speak for a long time, urgently calling on his listeners to be saved from that perverse generation. There were about three thousand men and women who responded positively to what he said, and they were all baptized into the name of Jesus in the ritual baths. The angels in heaven were rejoicing.

* * *

---

19. Psalm 110:1.

"When a child is born," Peter said, "you do not simply ignore it, hoping that somehow it will grow to maturity on its own. The same is true of a spiritual child. A spiritual child, like a natural child, needs love and food and nurturing."

"So, what are you saying?" John asked.

"I am saying that we need to teach these new disciples everything Jesus taught us."

"What do you have in mind?"

"Well, they have received the Holy Spirit just as we have, but now they need to learn how to live as followers of Jesus. Remember, Jesus taught us by example . . . he modelled life in the kingdom for us. So we need to each take a few of these new disciples and do with them what Jesus did with us."

"But that took three years, Peter," Andrew protested, "there are people here that need to return to their homes in Asia, North Africa, Italy, and elsewhere."

"Then we need to teach them as much as we can before they leave," Peter replied. "And perhaps we need to start thinking of visiting them in the future . . . or writing them letters."

"I think we need to compile a collection of Jesus's teaching," Matthew said.

"More than just teaching surely," Mary of Magdala added, "people need to know how Jesus fits into our story . . . into the story of the world."

"You mean like how his life and ministry fulfilled what the sages and prophets wrote about?" Matthew asked.

"Like when Jesus took us through Moses, the Psalms, and the Prophets . . . yes," Mary replied.

"But perhaps, even more," John added. "Perhaps we need to show how Jesus is God . . . where he came from . . . that was probably the hardest thing for me to learn."

"These are all wonderful suggestions, but I think we may be getting a little ahead of ourselves, here, brethren," Peter said. "For now they need to learn what we have learned. They are babies in Jesus, like we were once babies in Jesus. We must never forget how we once were. They need to know the Scriptures . . . that is priority. Everything else builds on that knowledge. They need to learn how to read it, memorize it, and inwardly digest it . . . to interpret it and apply it correctly with the help of the Holy Spirit. After all, he is the one who leads us in truth, yes?[20] And then, they need to learn how to worship in the absence of the sacrificial system . . . that is going to be very hard for some of them. They must also learn how to pray, how to really pray to the Father . . . that relational, yet relentless and persistent type of prayer . . . just like Jesus modelled for us,

---

20. John 16:13.

like he showed us. And we need to make sure they know and understand that they must live according to the principles Jesus taught."

"But what about their families?" Andrew asked.

"What about their families?"

"Many of their families are not believers in Jesus . . . yet. They need to learn how to tell them about him . . . to lead them to him, so that they might believe too."

"And," James added, "they will need to learn how to take care of each other . . . and of others outside their communities. Remember how they excommunicated the man born blind. I think we need to be ready for a number of excommunications in the future . . . and we must consider that it is possible that those who have relied on the synagogue for daily provision will be left destitute."

"May I say something?" It was Mary, John Mark's mother. She had been listening to their conversation with growing alarm, wringing her hands in worry.

"Yes, Mary, of course. What is it?" Peter replied.

"You cannot teach all three thousand here. My home . . . even the whole compound is too small."

Peter couldn't help but burst out laughing. "No, dear Mary. No, we cannot. We will need to take them out like Jesus took us out . . . to the Mount of Olives, or out into the countryside. We have enjoyed your hospitality and we are most grateful, but we would not dream of imposing on you any further than what we already have."

"I was beginning to worry," Mary said, breathing a sigh of relief. "Had you insisted, I would have asked one of you to begin multiplying the food!"

"Faith!" Andrew nearly yelled.

"What about faith?"

"We need to teach them how to exercise faith . . . not presumption, but faith. They will surely face impossible situations in the future, even as we did."

"Right now," Peter replied, "I think we need more faith than ever before just to start this process! But I suppose we will learn as we move forward, no?"

"May I say something more?" Mary asked again.

"Of course, Mary, please feel free to say whatever is on your heart. You do not need permission."

"Well, I was wondering if other Jerusalem residents would not be willing to open their homes for such meetings as you are proposing. Everyone can share in providing the meals . . . and those who are blessed with more can share with those who are in need. You don't all need to be together, do you? One apostle can go to each household."

"That's a wonderful idea, Mary!" Andrew exclaimed.

"And we can still worship at the temple every day," John reminded them. "That's where most people gather, anyway. So, we can teach there too . . . just like Jesus did."

"Just be careful, please," Mary cautioned, "things are not altogether settled yet. But right now, I think it is time for something to eat, yes?"

"You don't have to ask me twice," John said, standing up.

"Me neither," said Peter. "We twelve can continue to meet together on a daily basis . . . for prayers and for mutual encouragement. In the meantime, James, John, and Andrew . . . won't you three please find out who will be willing to open their homes for us to teach the new disciples."

"After breakfast . . ." Mary said.

"Indeed," Peter replied.

∗ ∗ ∗

3

The External Threat

I'm off to the temple for the afternoon prayers,"[1] John announced.

"I'm coming with you," Peter said.

The two disciples had become quite close since the trial. It was as if the failure of the one and the steadfastness of the other had drawn them into a deeper bond, an understanding of the unpredictable nature of humanity . . . there were no hidden secrets between them any longer. The trial and crucifixion had laid them bare, one to the other.

As they approached the gate that led from the court of the Gentiles into the court of women on the eastern side of the temple, the gate called Beautiful, a well-known beggar, a man crippled from birth, called out to them asking for money. Looking at the man, Peter remembered the words of his brother the day before. "Faith," Andrew had yelled out, "we need to teach them how to exercise faith . . . not presumption, but faith. They will surely face impossible situations in the future, even as we did."

"Why not?" Peter thought. Addressing the beggar, Peter said in an authoritative tone, "Look at us!" The man looked up with outstretched hands, expecting a coin to be placed in his open palm. "We do not have what you are asking for, we have neither silver nor gold . . . But we have something far better." Peter looked at John and smiled.

"Yes," John agreed, "something far better."

The man looked at them quizzically.

"In the name of Jesus Christ of Nazareth," Peter said loudly, "stand up and walk!"

---

1. There were three daily prayer times at the temple in the morning, the afternoon, and at sunset. "At the 'ninth hour' (i.e. three o'clock in the afternoon) the second Tamid was offered, the daily burnt offering that was sacrificed in early morning and in the evening (see Exod 29:38–42; Num 28:3–8)." Schnabel, *Acts*, 192.

He took the crippled man by the hand and helped him to his feet. The man's eyes were as big as a full moon. He could not believe that he was standing for the very first time in his life. At first, he held on to Peter . . . then he gave a step . . . then a small hop . . .

"I can . . . I can walk!" he said. Then he shouted out loudly, "I can walk!"

"Come, let us go in for the prayers," John urged.

The man accompanied them into the temple. He had never been allowed in before.[2] But, because of his overwhelming joy, he simply could not just walk in . . . he hopped, and he skipped, and he praised God as he went. The people around him recognized him and were amazed to see him there . . . walking and hopping and skipping. What had happened to him, they wondered?

Peter suddenly remembered the words of the prophet Isaiah, "See, your God is approaching to vindicate you, the reckoning of God; he is approaching to deliver you. He will open the eyes of the blind and unstop the ears of the deaf. He will cause the lame to frolic as the deer so that the dumb sing for pure joy. He will send water streams out in the wasteland."[3] Water . . . water that brings life . . . water that restores. Close to where they were standing at that moment, Jesus had cried out, "Those who are thirsty, ought to come to me and drink, for if you believe in me, know this: I am the one out of whom rivers of living waters will flow."[4]

The crowd began to grow, and Peter once more felt that inner compulsion to address them. "Why are you all so surprised?" he asked the awed onlookers, "As if we made this man walk by our own power or by our own righteousness? Our God . . . the God of Abraham, Isaac, and Jacob, the God of our ancestors . . . through this miracle done in the name of Jesus has vindicated and glorified his servant Jesus before your very eyes today. You gave him over to be killed . . . you rejected him before Pontius Pilate, a pagan man who declared Jesus innocent and wanted to let him go! But you scorned the Holy One . . . the Righteous One . . . and you asked for a brigand to be released in his place! You murdered the very author of life!"

Peter paused. Jesus had taught him to allow the people to process what they had heard . . . to allow them to see themselves laid bare and exposed by the truth . . . to see their hearts and their ways for what they were, before he provided them with the solution.

---

2. Leviticus 21:17–18; 2 Samuel 5:8.

3. Isaiah 35:4–6.

4. John 7:37–38.

"You disowned him . . . you rejected him . . . you did not receive him . . . and you murdered him! But God . . ." Peter paused once more. Then he shouted, "God raised him from the dead!"

There was a loud murmur in the crowd . . . some sighing, others gasping, a few scoffing, but Peter waved a hand indicating he had more to tell them. They fell silent.

"Yes, God raised Jesus from the dead. John and I are witnesses to this reality. And it is by faith in his name . . . it is faith in the name of Jesus, that has made this crippled man – this man whom you all know so well – faith in the name of Jesus, has made this man whole again. The name of Jesus . . . or more specifically, faith in the name of Jesus . . . is the power that has given him complete healing."

"As you can see!" cried the man, "Look! I can walk! I can jump!"

"My beloved brethren," Peter shouted above the growing noise of the crowd, "listen to me! I know you did this awful deed because you did not know any better . . . neither did your leaders. But this is the way God fulfilled what had been promised by the prophets . . . that the messiah would suffer in our place for our liberation from sin.[5] And so, I urge you all to repent, to turn away from evil . . . humble yourselves and turn back to God so that he might blot out your sins . . . so that you may be refreshed by the presence of the Lord Jesus who has been proclaimed to you."

"If Jesus has been raised from the dead, where is he now?" someone shouted from the crowd.

Without hesitation Peter replied, "Heaven has received him, where he will remain until the time of the restoration of all things,[6] which God promised long ago through his holy prophets."

"How do we know that Jesus is the one promised to us?" another voice shouted back.

"Moses told your fathers that one day God would send a prophet just like him from among your own brethren, remember?[7] He said you ought to pay attention to him. Every one that refuses to listen to him would be destroyed. From the time of Samuel, all the prophets announced what you have seen and heard in these days. You are sons and daughters of the prophets. You are members of the covenant God made with Abraham . . . remember when God promised Abraham that one day the whole world would be blessed through

---

5. Isaiah 53.

6. See 1 Corinthians 15:24–26; Psalm 110:1.

7. Deuteronomy 18:15–22.

his descendant?[8] Well, God has provided that descendant . . . that prophet . . . when God raised Jesus from the dead, he sent him first to you, to bless you by turning you away from your iniquities."

As Peter was still speaking to the crowd, the priests, the commander of the temple guards, and the Sadducees came up to them. Greatly disturbed by the proclamation that in Jesus the dead would be resurrected, they had both Peter and John arrested and thrown into prison for the night.[9] But about five thousand souls were added to the church that day because of Peter's preaching.

* * *

"Do you remember that hymn we sang the night Jesus was betrayed?"[10] John asked.

"Yes, I do," Peter replied. "How appropriate those words were for that night. My, how little we knew back then . . ." He turned to face John, "Do you know, I feel like I have learned more since Jesus died, than I learned in all the years before I met him . . . and even all the years while we walked with him . . . there was so much he said that I simply did not understand at the time."

"Could we sing that hymn now?" John persisted, "I think it would help me to deal with my anxious thoughts. Yes, yes, I know Jesus said we ought not to be anxious . . . that we ought not to be afraid . . . that we should exercise faith in him in the light of difficulties and struggles . . . but . . ."

"I know exactly what you mean . . . it is as if your head is at war with your heart, right?"

"Exactly. I remember him chiding us frequently for our lack of faith . . . we've been through so much, witnessed so much . . . his power over creation, over demons, over sickness . . . even over death itself. So . . . why then am I worried about tomorrow?"

"You are not alone, John. I've been sitting here wondering what Perpetua must be thinking tonight."

"Oh, I am so sorry . . . here I am being selfish and thinking only about myself."

8. Genesis 26:3–5; Galatians 3:16.

9. By law, any court proceeding ought to have been started and concluded in daylight hours.

10. Matthew 26:30; Mark 14:26. The hymn could have been Psalms 115–118, but it may have been something Jesus had taught them. Examples of early Christian hymnody can be found in various New Testament books and we also have the testimony of Pliny the Younger describing Christian practice of singing songs to "Christ as a god," in his epistle to Emperor Trajan.

"No, John . . . that's not why I mentioned Perpetua. I just wanted you to know that you are not alone in your doubts and fears. Besides, in one sense, doubts and fears are good things."

John looked quizzically at Peter, "How so?"

"Well, personally, it reminds me that I need him, that I cannot rely on myself . . . that I am dependent. Remember what I was like before I denied knowing him that night? I was so sure of myself."

"How could I forget," John replied, "we all were. Strange how you really only get to know yourself, the real you, when you suddenly face a catastrophe or a tragedy. All the pretence, the bravado, the projected image of self-control . . . all of that comes crashing down like a wall of mud in a rainstorm." He suddenly turned to look at Peter, an expression of concern on his face, "You do know that it is the same group of people before whom we will be standing tomorrow, yes? The same group of people who condemned Jesus to death."

"Yes . . . I realize that. But, you know, so much has happened since then, John. I can't quite explain it, but it is as if my natural inclination to worry and fret has been replaced with . . . with something else . . . a calmness . . . no, that's not it. A certainty."

"A security?" John asked.

"Yes . . . yes, that's a good word. Security . . . like I am being held together by something bigger than me . . . bigger, than the Sanhedrin . . . bigger than the world."

"Yes, I feel that too. Perhaps not quite as clearly as you. But you know what has really been bothering me? It's almost silly, but I was thinking about the fact that I am well acquainted with some in the high priest's family too."

"As strange as it may seem, John, I have been thinking about that as well. I remember, that's how you got me into the high priest's compound in the first place. I wonder what they will think about you now."

"That I am a sore disappointment, that's for sure . . . an embarrassment."

"You know, that night – that night in the high priest's compound – I was so very afraid that night, as you know. But Jesus . . . I remember watching him . . . he remained calm throughout the proceedings. In spite of all the awful things they said and did to him, he was at peace. Have you ever wondered how he could have faced them with such serenity?"

"Many times. Personally, I think it was because he knew the will of his father. He knew what had been planned all along. He knew what we did not know at the time." John sighed, "But I'm not sure we have that kind of knowledge tonight. I mean, I don't know what will happen tomorrow, do you?"

"No, I do not. But remember, Jesus did tell us that we would be persecuted . . . that we would be brought before councils and be judged and excommunicated . . . and that we ought not to be concerned because he would be with us.[11] But . . . and I've been thinking about this ever since we were arrested . . . he promised that the Holy Spirit would give us the words to speak when we need to say something.[12] So, I think we know more or less what will happen."

"More or less . . . perhaps . . . but not exactly."

"But again, that's why we need him . . . why we need to trust that he will do what he promised to do."

"And that is?"

"To give us a peace that transcends our understanding as well as the words to speak when we need to speak."

"And, I trust, to keep us quiet when we need to keep quiet too."

Peter laughed, "Yes, I need that."

"But the hymn . . ."

"Yes, the hymn. Let us sing it . . . it may lift our spirits and give us courage."

The two apostles sat side by side and together they sang the hymn Jesus had taught them. As they sang, the words brought back memories . . . things Jesus had said, things Jesus had done, and, as they had hoped, their spirits were lifted . . . not only lifted, but they soared. After they had completed the hymn, they sat in silence for a long while, each with their own thoughts.

Finally Peter said, "Before I met Jesus, I thought I knew the Scriptures . . . or at least, I thought I knew enough for a man like me . . . a fisherman . . . what more does a fisherman need to know than the basic Torah, right? But after our parents died and I took Andrew under my wing, I made sure he learned the Writings and the Prophets, not just the Torah. Somehow, I wanted him to know more than me . . . I wanted him to be better than me . . . I wanted to give him the opportunities I never had."

"You are like a father to him."

"Yes, more a father than a brother. I think at times in the past he resented that . . . especially when I tried to discipline him, or the times when he felt I was being overly protective."

"Like when he was struggling to forgive James and me for our superior attitudes?"

---

11. Isaiah 41:10; Matthew 10:17–20; 28:20; Mark 13:11; Luke 12:11–12; 21:12–19; John 15:26–16:4; Acts 18:10.

12. Luke 12:12.

"Yes," Peter chuckled as he remembered the unpleasant confrontation on the shore of the Sea of Galilee. "He really did not appreciate my interference. But, you know, our relationship was never only a one-way relationship. I learned so much from him . . . I still do. Just the other day, he took me through the entire prophecy of Joel."

"That came in handy the next day, didn't it?"

"It did." Peter sucked in a deep breath and then breathed out slowly, "You know, I used to struggle to memorize the Scriptures . . . but that day . . . that day, it was as if what I had learned before came flooding back . . . as clear as living water . . . like a sustained flash of lightening. I really don't know where that came from . . . sure, Jesus taught us so much during those forty days before he ascended. It was like drinking from a gushing spring after the rains! But it all seemed to fall into place in a very short time."

"Don't forget that you now have the Holy Spirit of God living in you . . . we all do. The same Spirit who inspired the sages of old to write the Holy Scriptures. Jesus said he would bring to mind all the things he taught us."[13]

"Exactly!" Peter excitedly grasped John's shoulder. "That is why we need not be fearful of what tomorrow may bring. We have him living in us . . . he will give us what we lack . . . what we cannot produce ourselves."

"Thank you . . . thank you, Peter. I needed to hear that. You know, after all this time, I think I am still learning . . . there is so much I do not know."

"You are not alone, John, you need to know that . . . you are not alone. I feel like that too. I think that's why Jesus always likened our relationship with him in terms of a journey, of walking . . . because we need that forward momentum, that forward movement . . . one small step before the other, and every step we take we learn more about life . . . about life in him.[14] It's so different to the life we lived before, it's like a daily adventure, don't you think?"

"I've never thought about it that way, but yes, I can see that. But for me, it sometimes feels like I'm walking in the dark . . . although I do have confidence as long as I walk as he walked . . . as long as I do what he did . . . because deep down inside, I think I know that even the darkness is like day to him. You know, like the Psalmist says, even though I walk through the dark valley of death, I know you are with me . . . there is evidence of his presence. I can't explain it, but I know it . . . in my heart."

---

13. John 16:13–15.
14. John 12:35–36; 1 John 1:7; 2:6.

"Well, Jesus did promise to never leave us . . . that he would be with us even to the end of time."[15]

"And therein lies our confidence . . . our faith . . . believing that what he said, he will do."

"Well put, John."

"Excuse me," a voice came to them out of the darkness. Somewhere outside their cell. The voice was garbled, as if the man's mouth was swollen. "Forgive me for interrupting, but I couldn't help listening to what you were saying. I am fearful for tomorrow as well. I don't know what they will do with me."

"Do you know the man we were talking about? Do you know who Jesus is?" Peter asked their unseen guest.

The man hesitated, "I thought I knew him once . . . many years ago. But recently I have heard a lot of rumours about him. Who hasn't? There has been so much talk in Jerusalem since his followers claimed he is not dead, but alive."

"But do you know him?" Peter persisted.

"No . . . no, I cannot say I do. I know about him, but I do not know him, although from what I have heard you two saying tonight, I would very much like to know him. It seems like he has changed the way you look at life."

"Then I will tell you more about him so that you might come to really know him as we know him." Peter went on to tell the man about Jesus – starting from the time he first met him. John added a few details here and there as he went along. Then the three men sat and spoke with each other for a long time, the man in the darkness asked many questions, and Peter and John answered him.

"And so here we are now, imprisoned for healing a lame man in the name of Jesus, the Nazarene," Peter concluded.

There was silence for a moment. Then they heard the sound of gentle weeping. "I too am from Nazareth," the man sobbed, "that is where I met Jesus. I was acquainted with the family. But I did not believe in him then. I was one that helped cast him out of the synagogue . . . my hand was with them when they tried to push him over that cliff. We were convinced he was a charlatan . . . a blasphemer."

"And now?" John asked.

Without wavering the man said, "I believe Jesus is the Messiah . . . I believe everything you have told me. The witness of your lives . . . only the truth could set you free from the past . . . only the truth could give you confidence to face an uncertain future. As you have said, Jesus fulfilled all what the prophets said about the messiah. To be honest, I did not think the messiah would be crucified

---

15. Matthew 28:20; John 14:18, 23.

and die . . . no one taught us to expect a suffering, servant type messiah . . . nor a single resurrection, for that matter. All I was taught, was that there would be a general resurrection of all the dead at the end of time. But you have made it abundantly clear to me that this too was a fulfilment of what the Scriptures teach us. So, yes, I believe . . . I believe that Jesus is the Lord."

"Ah, how the angels are rejoicing," Peter said. "Welcome, brother! Welcome to the flock of Jesus."

"Would you mind singing that hymn again, please?" the man said, "I'd like to take the words with me as I face my accusers tomorrow."

"And then we will pray for each other, yes?" John suggested.

"Yes," Peter said. Then he began to sing . . . slowly, so that the man could hear every word and sing with them. And then they prayed.

* * *

The Sanhedrin, made up of the rulers, elders, and experts of the law, gathered together in Jerusalem. Both Annas and Caiaphas were present,[16] as well as John,[17] Alexander,[18] and other men of the high priest's family.

Peter and John had bid their prison companion farewell earlier that morning. In the light of the dawn, they saw that he had been badly beaten by his captors. As the guards led him away, Peter heard him softly singing the words of the hymn they had sung during the night. He had professed faith in Jesus and testified that he was no longer fearful of what his accusers would do to him. He had expressed repentance of his violent past as a zealot and was prepared to face the consequences. In life or in death, he had said, he would be obedient to Jesus.

The guards came and led Peter and John to where the Sanhedrin was assembled. John thought one of the guards looked familiar, he was clearly Jewish . . . but there were other things on his mind, so he said nothing. Yet he noted that there was a gentleness about the man . . . and a nervousness. Was he one of the guards in the garden? . . . The high priest's courtyard? . . . The cross? . . . The tomb?

---

16. Annas was high priest from AD 6 to AD 15. While five of his sons held the office after him, his son-in-law, Joseph Caiaphas, served as high priest during the trial of Jesus. Yet Annas apparently still had great authority.

17. Some believe this man to be Johanan ben Zacchai, the president of the Great Synagogue after its removal to Jamnia, but precise identification remains uncertain. Cf. Knowling, *Acts of the Apostles*, 125.

18. Identity unknown.

Peter noticed the crowds gathering along the way. Some were shouting words of encouragement, others questioning the reason for their arrest and imprisonment.

As the doors opened and the disciples walked in, they both felt a flood of confidence sweep over them. Peter looked at John and smiled. The Holy Spirit was definitely present and doing what Jesus had said he would do.

To the side of the room stood the healed lame beggar. Peter noticed that the leaders still had no compassion – they made him, who had never stood, stand in a corner. But pure joy radiated from his face. There was such serenity . . . such a look of peace. The man had received more than healing . . . he had received salvation, life eternal in Jesus.

The murmur in the room stopped abruptly and one of the members of the Sanhedrin turned to face the disciples. He glared at them for a long while. Peter assumed this was an attempt to intimidate them.

Pointing at the healed man, their accuser said, "By what authority . . . in whose name . . . how did you do this . . . this . ." The man was clearly trying to avoid the word miracle, so he said nothing further.

Peter felt a warm surge of courage wash over him. He opened his mouth to speak and was pleasantly surprised when he spoke freely and boldly, "Leaders and rulers of our people. Are we being questioned today because of an act of kindness shown to a lame man? Do you wish to know how he was healed? Then I will tell you . . . you and all our people. He was healed in the name of Jesus Christ the Nazarene."

A strange hissing sound filled the room, as if every man had sucked in air through their teeth at the same time. Some of the members of the Sanhedrin were clearly uncomfortable at the mention of Jesus's name, as they shifted in their seats and made dismissive movements with their hands.

"Yes, Jesus . . . the same man you condemned to be crucified," Peter pressed on, "but whom God vindicated by raising him from the dead! It is through faith in his name that this man stands before you . . . completely healed."

John could not believe his ears. Was this the same Peter who had denied the Lord for fear of being condemned himself? And from where did that eloquence come?

"Jesus is the stone rejected by the builders, but, as the Psalmist said, he has now become the cornerstone[19] of our faith. Salvation is to be found in no one else. There is no other name given under heaven by which we may be saved . . . only the name of Jesus."

---

19. Psalm 118:22.

John was not the only one in the room taken aback by Peter's defence. The Sanhedrin appeared to be stunned, like oxen hit hard between the eyes with a wooden post. Who were these men? Were they not ordinary fishermen? Not one of the teachers of the law claimed them as their students. But where did they gain such knowledge? From that peasant rabbi, Jesus? They could not refute what Peter had said because the healed man was standing right there for all to see.

Annas indicated that the guards should remove Peter and John from the room so that the members of the Sanhedrin might speak to each other in private. As they were leaving Peter heard them asking each other what they ought to do with them, because the whole of Jerusalem knew about the miracle . . . a miracle they could not deny. As the doors closed behind them, they heard one member shout out that they ought to be prevented from ever speaking to anyone in "that" name . . . could they not even say the name of Jesus?

"May I speak with you two, privately?" one of their guards asked in a hushed voice.

"You look familiar," John said as they moved off to one side.

"I was wondering if you recognized me," the guard replied.

"Were you one of the temple guards posted to keep watch over Jesus's tomb?"

"Yes, I was . . . I was also one of those paid to spread the lie that his followers . . . that you stole his body during the night. How I have regretted my cowardice since then!"

Peter looked at the man standing before him. He remembered wondering where the guards were when he and John went to the tomb that day.

"You used the word, 'lie,'" John said in an enquiring tone.

"Yes . . . I didn't believe it then, and I don't believe it now. We all saw that angel . . ."

"What angel?" Peter asked.

"There was an angel that opened the tomb," the guard replied.

"Did you know that, John?"

"No, I did not . . . I wonder why Jesus never told us. Ah, no matter. Now we know."

"I didn't know about you being paid to lie about Jesus's resurrection either," Peter said.

"Forgive me," the guard replied, looking embarrassed, "but our lives were in danger and . . ."

"And so you denied him too," Peter said.

"Excuse me? No, I lied about him . . . I lied about what we saw."

"I believe what Peter is trying to say is that there is something you two have in common. On the night of the trial, Peter was afraid . . . afraid that the mob might kill him if they found out he was one of Jesus's followers."

"So, I denied that I ever knew Jesus," Peter added. "We basically committed the same sin, don't you see? You lied about him . . . I denied him, which was also a lie. In short, we both failed him."

"I understand," the guard said, "but here you are now, speaking boldly in his name . . . how did you ever deal with your lie . . . with your denial . . . with your sin? I spoke to your former fellow prisoner this morning. He told me what you said last night, he was witnessing to me about Jesus, about what Jesus means to him since he met you two . . . and I was wondering . . . is there hope for me? Is there forgiveness for what I have done?"

"There is always hope with God," John said emphatically. "And there is always forgiveness with our God . . . even though your sin may be great, his grace is greater still."

"If you confess your sin and turn to Jesus, you too may become one of his children . . . and you are welcome to join our community," Peter added smiling.

"You would welcome me?" the guard said doubtfully.

"As a fellow believer? Yes, without hesitation," Peter replied. "But tell me . . . our fellow prisoner. What happened to him?"

The guard swallowed hard. He clearly looked distressed. Then he replied, "I'm afraid he was executed earlier this morning. But I must hasten to tell you that he went to his death with praise on his lips. He was singing a hymn . . ."

"The hymn we taught him last night," John said. "Ah, Lord Jesus, we commit your child to your care. Receive him in paradise this day."

"And receive our brother here as well. Strengthen him and—"

"Forgive me," the guard interrupted. Then suddenly taking on a false, gruff tone of voice he said, "You two must go back in. They are calling you back." Adding under his breath, "May I come to talk with you later?"

"Yes," Peter said, "we must pray for you, that you too may be filled with the promise."

"The promise?" The guard was pushing them along roughly and yet gently.

"You will see. In the meantime, stay safe. The leaders will not take kindly to the change that has taken place in your life today."

The guard led them back into the courtroom.

The same man as before stood up and told them the decision of the group was unanimous. They were to refrain from speaking to anyone or teaching anyone in the name of Jesus.

John could not hold back. He was known to the high priest,[20] and for a moment their eyes connected. "Surely none of you believe that it is better before God to obey you than him! You are asking us to suppress the truth! But we cannot deny what we have both seen and heard for ourselves."

"We will punish you if you do not do as we command!" one member shouted. There were a number of similar threats yelled out by others as well, but they simply could not agree on what kind of punishment would be appropriate because the people, whose loud protests could be heard from outside, had witnessed the miraculous healing of a man over the age of forty, and they were outraged by the arrest and imprisonment.

The high priest dismissed them with a wave of his hand. On their way out, the guard agreed to meet with them later in the day. The lame man, whose name they discovered was Asher, also met them and asked if he might accompany them to join the others. Peter noticed that he still walked with a hop and a skip in each step.

"Absolutely," John said, "you are now one of us, whether you like it or not!"

But there was another familiar face waiting to greet them as they left the building.

"Peter," the young man said, "do you remember me?"

Peter looked at the young man's face. He knew him, but he wasn't completely sure, "Not really. Where did we meet?"

"In the garden on the Mount of Olives. You admirably defended Jesus with your small sword."

"Oh!" Peter exclaimed, blushing profusely as he recognized the man. "You are the servant whose ear I cut off[21] . . . I am so sorry. Please forgive me. I was so afraid at the time, and I had promised to—"

"Please," the man stopped Peter. "There is no need to apologize. I would have done the same given the circumstances. Besides, Jesus healed me, remember? And I have believed in him ever since then. I could not deny what he did for me, so I believe . . . as do my family and my friends. I shared with them what happened and what Jesus did, now we all believe in him."

"You . . . you *believe*? You *all* believe?" Peter asked.

"Yes. Also, I have been listening to your preaching . . . and I listened to what you both said in there. I want to know more. Will you teach me so I can continue to teach my family and my friends?"

"Will I? But of course! Are you able to come with us right now?"

---

20. John 18:15–16.

21. Luke 22:50–51; John 18:10–11.

"If I may?"

"You most certainly may. You are more than welcome. But may we know your name?" John asked.

"My name is Malchus."[22]

"Well, welcome, Malchus!" Peter said. "Welcome, brother. Come . . . we have to tell the others. They must be worried about us."

The four believers chatted as they walked, the overjoyed crowd thronging about them. So much had happened in the past few hours. They had seen the Holy Spirit at work in their lives and in the lives of others . . . and heaven was all the richer for it.

* * *

They knocked on the gate and called for Rhoda to open the door. She nearly bowled them over for joy. The girl really was a little overly enthusiastic at times. Then again, she was still very young.

"Peter! John!" Mark ran up to greet the apostles, "Thank the Lord you are safe! We have been praying ever since we heard. Oh"—Mark was suddenly aware of the two strangers with Peter and John—"forgive me. You two must think I am very rude. I'm John Mark."

"I am Asher," the previously lame man replied awkwardly. He was not yet used to being received at public gatherings.

"And I am Malchus. I'm a friend of Peter," Malchus smiled a toothy smile.

Peter blushed a little, "I . . . uhm . . . I relieved Malchus of his ear in the garden."

"But only for a brief moment," Malchus chuckled, "then Jesus restored it to its rightful place."

"Peter! John!" Mary came to greet them, "Oh, you two are a welcome sight for my old eyes. We are all assembled . . . we've been praying for you. Come. We have three new members for you to meet! Isn't it exciting?"

Peter and John first introduced their two new brothers to Mary, and then followed her to the upper room where many members of the community were gathered together. There were three darker skinned men standing talking with James to one side. When Peter and John entered, James led them over to meet them.

"Peter, John . . . welcome back! I'm sure you are going to tell us all about your . . . your, uhm . . ." James began to tear up.

---

22. Matthew 26:51; Mark 14:47; Luke 22:50–51; John 18:10–11. That Malchus is named suggests possible conversion to the Way.

"Adventure?" John offered, smiling.

"Brother!" James snuffled, flinging his arms around his younger sibling. He was barely able to control his emotions. "If anything had happened to you, I would never have forgiven myself."

There was a cry from the doorway. Peter turned to see first Perpetua and then Salome rushing towards them. Both their faces were wet with tears . . . their eyes were red and swollen. They had been weeping a long time.

"My precious husband!" Perpetua held Peter tightly. He leaned into her warmth. How he loved her!

"My son! My sons!" Salome was less restrained, hugging both her sons, wailing loudly.

"Mother . . ." James said, embarrassed, struggling to free himself from her smothering embrace. "I was just going to introduce . . ."

"No," said the older dark-skinned man, "no, leave her be. Allow her to show you her heart. You will miss that one day."

The man's two sons' eyes were moist. "Indeed," they said almost in unison. Then the one continued, "Our mother passed on two years ago. We miss her hugs now more than ever."

Salome looked at the two young men . . . then letting go of her own sons she hugged the two of them instead.

Mary, the mother of Jesus entered the room. She walked over to Peter and John and greeted them. "I now understand why Simeon spoke about a sword piercing my heart. Forgive me, but I must confess I relived the terror of my own long, dark night." Turning to John she said, "Your mother felt the same anguish I did . . . she loves you both very much." Then turning to the older dark-skinned man, she said to Peter and John, "May I introduce a man who means so very much to me. Peter, John, this is Simon. He comes from Cyrene in North Africa. And these are his two sons, Alexander and Rufus. It was Simon who helped Jesus carry the cross beam."[23]

"I am so very pleased to make your acquaintance," Peter said, kissing the man on both cheeks and hugging him tightly.

"As am I . . ." Simon said. "I've always had a fascination with people named Simon."

They all laughed.

"But we call him Peter now," Mark blurted out, immediately regretting attracting attention to himself.

Peter ruffled his hair.

---

23. Matthew 27:32; Mark 15:21; Luke 23:26; Romans 16:13; Acts 11:20.

"Don't," Mark said, "please, don't . . . I'm not a little boy anymore."

"Indeed, you are not!" Peter said. "Quite the man of the house. And one whom I love as my own son."

"Peter!" Matthew yelled from the other side of the room, "Are you going to keep us in suspense all day long?"

Peter clapped his hands together, indicating that he wanted to speak, "First, may I introduce to you all, Malchus. He has been a believer since the night our Lord was betrayed . . . or to be more precise, from the moment Jesus gave him back the ear I lopped off." Everyone laughed.

"Welcome, Malchus!" they cried.

"And this is our new brother, Asher," John said. "Jesus healed him yesterday and we got thrown into prison for it!"

"Welcome, Asher! And thank you, Jesus!"

"And, I am assuming you have all had an opportunity to visit with Simon and his sons, Alexander and Rufus from North Africa." Turning to Simon, he said, "It is so good to have you all with us."

Peter then proceeded to tell them about their night in prison . . . about their encounter with the former zealot from Nazareth and his subsequent encounter with Jesus prior to his execution that morning. He told them about the guard . . . about the Sanhedrin and their ugly threats.

"I know the high priest's family well," John added; "they will not relent."

Peter also told them that the Holy Spirit had not only been present with them throughout the trial, but he had also given them boldness and courage.

"And he gave Peter the words to speak, just as Jesus promised!" John shouted above the loud praises of joy and thanks to God.

"Sovereign Lord!" Matthew prayed, "You created all things and sustain all in existence. By the inspiration of the Holy Spirit you said through your servant David: 'Why do the nations assemble and plot futile things? Kings and rulers rise and conspire together against the Lord and his anointed one.' All this was fulfilled in our lifetime, Father. Herod . . . Pontius Pilate . . . both Jews and Gentiles met together to plot against your holy and anointed servant Jesus. And yet, they could only do what you had planned all along."

"Yes, Father," Mary continued, "and now they have threatened your servants, as you said they would. Consider their words and their actions and grant us all more boldness in the face of their hostility so that we might witness even more to the truth!"

"Continue to stretch out your hands, too, dear Lord," Malchus prayed, "to heal and do signs of wonder in the holy name of your servant Jesus!"

Suddenly the whole house shook. Peter first thought that it was another earthquake, but then he felt that familiar warmth within and he knew the Holy Spirit was present in power. He sensed a greater confidence rising within him . . . God was with them . . . amid the uncertainty of their present situation, of that he was certain.

* * *

4

The Internal Threat

I know there are some who are struggling financially," Joseph said. "I had a small piece of land, but I no longer need it. So, I have sold it . . . but I don't need the money either. Now, please, take this and distribute it among those who are needy."[1]

"That is most generous, Joseph," Peter said, "but I thought Levites were not meant to own land?"[2] Peter smiled and lifted his eyebrows in mock reprimand. Mary was Joseph's aunt and he was well known to their community.

"Ah! A law expert!" Joseph joked. "I think that law was largely ignored from the time of the Babylonian exile on."

"I am only joking," Peter said, suddenly sorry he had said anything at all. "Thank you for your gift. I know a few families in Jerusalem that will benefit from your kindness."[3]

"You are all doing such wonderful work . . . I want to help in any way I can. My own aunt has set an example for me by opening her house to you for your gatherings.[4] Besides, the Lord exhorts us through the prophet not to live in fine houses while his temple lies in ruins, not so?"[5]

"She has set an example for us all," Peter added. "Tell me, just out of curiosity, what do you do? I mean, what do you do well . . . naturally?"

---

1. Deuteronomy 15:4, 11.

2. Numbers 18:20; Deuteronomy 10:9; Joshua 13:33.

3. "There is no hint that the apostles solicited or coerced these donations, but they do appear to have complete control over their distribution. In this capacity, the apostles direct their efforts exclusively to meeting the material needs of everyone in the community, in marked contrast to the exploitive practices of temple officials and other well-known 'lovers of money' (Lk. 16:14)." Spencer, *Journeying through Acts*, 65–66.

4. See Colossians 4:10 where Barnabas is said to be the cousin of John Mark, the son of Mary.

5. Haggai 1:4.

"I am an encourager."

Peter had not expected such a reply, "An encourager?"

"Yes. It is a gift I've always had, even when I was young. Of course, I want to do more, I'd like to help distribute aid and visit people, if I may . . . but you asked what I do well . . . and that is what I do best. I encourage people, encourage them to face whatever trials they are facing, encourage them to press on when they are discouraged. I always see the best in others . . . I see what they can be if someone would only believe in them and take the time to invest in them, and I capitalize on that."

"Something you and Jesus have in common," Peter replied. "He saw in me what I did not see in myself, and he built on that . . . at times it was as if he did not see my faults, or, at least, he did not dwell on them. You know, it was Jesus who gave me the name Peter . . . and that on the very first day he met me!" He paused, savouring the memory, then he added, "I think we will call you Barnabas. Son of encouragement."

"That's an excellent name for an excellent cousin," Mark said walking in at that moment.

"John Mark!" Barnabas said embracing his cousin. "Here's a young man I would love to work with . . . he has one of the most gentle hearts I have ever encountered . . . not to mention his brilliant mind." Barnabas ruffled his hair.

"Don't . . . please don't," Mark said.

"But you have hair that says, 'ruffle me' . . . I can't help it."

"It seems no one can help it. People are forever ruffling my hair. And sometimes their hands aren't clean!" Mark whined, jokingly.

"I think you two would be great together," Peter interjected. "Mark why not show Barnabas the homes where all the other believers meet. I think it might be best to distribute any aid we receive equally among the communities themselves. That way, each group will help their own members."

"You've received other gifts as well?" Barnabas asked.

"Yes," Peter replied, "it seems the Holy Spirit has given us all the same heart and mind. Everyone shares with others . . . we're like one big, caring family."

"And, I hear, the whole community actively witnesses about Jesus wherever they go," Barnabas said. "They are really walking in your footsteps, Peter. You are such a good example to us all."

"Oh, you great son of encouragement . . . now you are laying it on a bit too thick. But thank you. I am indebted to the work of the Holy Spirit in that regard. Truly, I don't think I would do half of what I'm doing now if he was not with me and in me!"

"And he's far less grumpy," Perpetua said as she walked in.

"I used to be grumpy, you say?" Peter looked up at his wife, smiling.

"And oh so moody . . . you really gave Andrew a hard time when he came to tell you that he had found the messiah."

"That is true," Peter said. "I was filled with fear . . . for him . . . and I was disillusioned."

"Life was so different then," Perpetua added, "we had such different priorities and values . . . or, at least, I did. My husband, my daughter, our business . . . all that came first. Now, I just want people to know the freedom we have in Jesus."

"Well, the word is certainly spreading," Barnabas said.

"And, I suspect, the opposition," Mark chimed in.

"Now who is being grumpy and moody?" Peter teased.

"Mark is right, though," Perpetua said, "we must not be caught unawares like this last time. I was sick with worry that night."

"I think we all know what to expect next time," Peter said. "But we must be watchful and prayerful . . . that's what Jesus told me the night he was betrayed. If I'd only listened—"

"Then you would not have learned as much as you did," Perpetua interrupted. "And we would not have learned from you, either."

"It seems we have a daughter of encouragement here," Barnabas joked.

"Ah, yes, so we do," Peter said rising to embrace his wife. "Where would I be without you, my dear Perpetua?"

"Ah, Barnabas?" Mark said, blushing slightly. "I think now would be a good time to show you the other homes where our brethren meet."

* * *

"What?" Peter felt a sense of panic rising within him. Being threatened by the Sanhedrin was one thing, it was external. But this was a threat from within their own ranks.

"Here are witnesses.[6] They were in the gate when the contract was ratified and when the sum was paid in full," Philip said.

The witnesses told the assembly what they had seen and heard.

---

6. "A land transaction was basically carried out in four steps: writing the document, signature of the witnesses, sealing the document, and storing the document." See *Cultural Backgrounds Study Bible* comment on Jeremiah 32:9–10; (44), 1283–84.

"Why would they do such a thing? It is like a false scale . . . this is an abomination to our Lord!"[7] Peter was horrified that such a vile lie could have come from a member of their own community. "It is the sin of covetousness."

"It is worse than that," Andrew stated. "It is like the sin of Achan.[8] Ananias and Sapphira have brought trouble on our whole community. Soon all of Jerusalem will be wagging their tongues against us. They will say we are no better than the pagans . . . that we have no regard for the law, or for holy living, for that matter. We must confront them and deal with this matter quickly."

"You are sure that Sapphira knew about this? She is not an innocent victim, is she? I don't know them well . . ."

"No, she knew. But Peter, I really don't want to repeat the gossip. It would be better if you asked her yourself."

For a moment Peter sat silently contemplating what course of action he ought to take. That a brazenly barefaced sin had been committed was obvious. What were they thinking? Surely, they could not have believed that the truth would not come to light sooner or later. The sale of their property had been done in the open, and the contract signed before witnesses. Did they try to make others complicit in their falsehood? How many people were involved in this affair? Or was this something they decided on their own? Just between the two of them? But their arrogant selfishness would harm the community as a whole, their lie would reflect negatively on the honesty of the rest of the believers . . . and the name of Jesus would be disgraced.

"Perhaps they will repent . . . there may yet be a way for them to make atonement and restitution . . . and to clear their names," Peter stated, almost under his breath.

"And our name as a community," Philip said. "Such an action could be dangerous for us all should the Sanhedrin come to hear about it."

"And our Lord's name too," Andrew added. "Let's not forget that the action of those who bear his name disgraces him as well."

"Have them sent to me," Peter said to Philip. He told the witnesses to stand outside the door at the back of the room until he summoned them. Then turning to Andrew he said, "How I loathe confrontation. I am only beginning to understand how difficult it must have been for Jesus to confront me . . . but this . . . this is on a different level. This is not well-intentioned ignorance. This

---

7. Proverbs 11:1.
8. Joshua 7.

is not of the Holy Spirit . . . this is from the father of lies himself. Satan has slithered into the very midst of our community."

"O sovereign Lord," Andrew prayed, laying a hand on his brother's shoulder, "grant your servant, Peter, great wisdom and grace as he deals with the wickedness that has risen in our community. Two of our own have foolishly thought that you do not see what is done in secret. Rise up, O God, and purge the people of your choosing. Do not reject us because of the sins of others . . . do not withhold your presence as you did with Joshua because of the sin of Achan. Bring to light the corruption, the lies, the hypocrisy, and the covetousness, so that it may be removed from our midst."

"Amen," Peter said. "Amen. So be it . . . thank you. Ah, here he comes."

Ananias walked in and stood before Peter. Peter looked into his eyes. There was no sign of guilt or shame that he could discern. But he wanted to give him the benefit of the doubt and so he said, "Brother, you gave us quite a large sum of money from the sale of your property."

"Yes, we did, didn't we? So many others were selling their properties and giving the proceeds to you for distribution among the less fortunate . . . it was the least we could do."

"Ananias, you do realize that the land was yours to do with as you pleased, yes? And after the sale, the money was yours to do with as you wished . . . to keep all, give all, or divide it as you saw fit. You do know that, correct? Our community does not require members to donate money or land or houses . . . if you give, you give out of the goodness of your heart."

"And that is what we did."

"And you said you gave us the same sum you were paid for the land . . . I am correct, yes?"

"Yes . . . Peter, why all these questions?" Ananias asked irritably. "I don't recall you asking Barnabas any questions . . . nor anyone else, for that matter. Is our money not good enough for you? Was it not enough?"

"Still you persist in your lie," Peter said, trying to control the feeling of anger rising within him. "Here are witnesses, Ananias . . . witnesses who know the truth!"

Andrew brought in the witnesses. Peter saw Ananias swallow hard and turn pale.

"How is it possible that you have opened your heart to Satan, Ananias?" Peter questioned. "Do you really think God is blind?"

"How dare you . . . you have lent out your ears to the gossipers."

"Not so!" Peter thundered. "You thought you could get away with your deception. But you have not lied to mortals . . . you have lied to God!"[9]

Ananias opened his mouth as if to protest, but no sound came out of it. His legs buckled under him and he fell to the floor. Andrew ran over to him and rolled him over.

"He's dead, brother."

At first Peter was rendered immobile and mute . . . he did not know what to do or what to say. He had not expected lies from a fellow believer, but he had not expected him to drop down dead either. "How very, very tragic," he said softly. "I wish he had repented. But now, God has made his evil recoil upon his own head. What does the Scripture say? 'Vengeance is Mine, says the Lord.'"[10] Peter looked up at his brother now standing over the lifeless body of Ananias. "You were right, you know. This is exactly like the sin of Achan."

Peter stood up slowly . . . he felt like a great weight was pressing him down. What had just happened? What would he say to the rest of the group? The horrified witnesses stood stock-still behind him. He walked over to where Andrew still stood, wide-eyed and motionless. This was all so sudden. But if their witness to Jesus was to mean anything to the nonbelievers, they had to demonstrate a steady and uncompromising loyalty to the moral and ethical principles and values taught by Jesus. The sin of Ananias was not merely an innocent or even ignorant miscalculation. He deliberately and persistently sought to deceive others to make himself appear to be better than them. In a community based on truth, integrity was essential. He knew that.

"God has struck him down like he struck down Nadab and Abihu.[11] Like them, Ananias offered an unholy gift to the Lord. Have the younger men take him to the field for burial," Peter said, sighing deeply. "Although I am profoundly grieved, we may not mourn for him."[12]

Together with the witnesses, Andrew left, glad to be rid of the awful sight. He felt he needed to clear his mind. Peter sat down heavily, his head resting in his hands. He looked up when he heard the young men come in, half hoping that he would not see what he clearly did. He instructed them to wrap the

---

9. "Lying to God insinuates that God is not all-knowing, that God can be deceived. In effect, this denies that God is God! Dishonesty and impure motives in Christians can also hinder others from coming to faith in Christ, of which Paul was keenly aware (2 Cor 4:2; 1 Thess 2:3)." Kurz, *Acts of the Apostles*, 93–94.

10. Deuteronomy 32:35.

11. Leviticus 10.

12. Jeremiah 16:5–7.

body in a burial shroud and carried him out. A deep sense of reverential fear descended on all those present.

Peter excused himself for the moment. He needed time to reflect on what had happened and to pray before meeting with Sapphira.

Three hours later, she came up from the marketplace. She was in a jovial mood, jingling her gold bangles and tossing her braided hair about her shoulders as she walked.

"Why the long faces?" she purred as she walked into the room, looking first at Andrew and then at Peter.

Peter was in no mood to be toyed with. He felt wrung out like an old dry washcloth. "Tell me, Sapphira. The money you gave for distribution to the needy in our community . . . did you give the full amount you received from the sale of your property?"

"But of course, Peter," Sapphira twirled her string of pearls between her fingers, swaying her hips from side to side.

"Not even a blush," Peter said quietly. He rose and stood before her. "How could you have conspired with your husband to test the Holy Spirit of God? I had hoped you were ignorant of his lies, but now I see you have the same wicked spirit in you."

Sapphira clenched her teeth but said nothing. Chin up, her eyes blazed with anger and defiance.

"Listen!" Peter said to her, pointing to the door. "Do you hear? The feet of those who have buried your husband are at the door . . . they have come in time to carry you out as well."

Sapphira drew in a sharp breath. "Buried?" A look of terror and bewilderment clouded her face. Then she too fell down at his feet. She was dead.

Peter turned away slowly. "God has no pleasure in the death of the wicked,"[13] he said. "How I wish they had repented . . ."

"This is a sad day for our community," Andrew added.

"Yes. But there is a lesson for us in this. We must be on our guard at all times. Just because people call Jesus Lord, does not mean they know him. Didn't Jesus say something like that once?"

"Yes, he said that there would be some who would call him Lord, but not do the things he taught. Wolves clothed like sheep . . . they only enter the fold to destroy the flock. But what has happened will reach the ears of many . . . and they will fear the Lord. They will think twice before joining our community under false pretences."

---

13. Ezekiel 18:23; 33:11.

"Greed," Peter said, almost to himself, "it is the age-old tool of our adversary. Satan tempted Jesus with an offer of kingdoms.[14] He tempted Judas with silver.[15] And now he seeks to trip us up by infiltrating our own community! I am sorry for the deaths of Ananias and Sapphira, but at least the flock has been spared any further grief. For that I am grateful."

"You are a rock, brother. Our Lord chose well."

"You know, this is the part about tending the lambs that I do not enjoy at all."

"Come, let us walk out to the Mount of Olives."

"Yes. That will be helpful. Thank you."

* * *

---

14. Luke 4:5–8.

15. Luke 22:3–6.

5

Whom to Obey

"But things have been going so well," Thomas complained. "We've been meeting openly in Solomon's Colonnade. True, some are too afraid to join us because of the awful incident with Ananias and Sapphira, but many others are turning to the Lord. People even line the streets with their sick waiting for Peter to pass by . . . I've personally seen a number of people healed just by being touched by his shadow. Clearly the Lord is with us . . . so many sick and demon-possessed people finding relief and release. Why now, Matthew, why now?"

"I don't know, Thomas. But John has contacts, and they told him the Sanhedrin is planning on arresting all of us. Apparently, they are jealous of the sheer numbers coming over to our community."

"All of us?"

"Yes. All of us."

"Well, we can't hide in fear of something that may never happen, can we?"

"No, we can't . . . and we shouldn't. God has not given us a spirit of fear,[1] Jesus told us not to be anxious . . . not even when they persecute us."[2]

"So, shall we join the others? I believe we are meant to be teaching again at the time of the afternoon prayers."

"Yes. Let's go."

* * *

The apostles gathered together in the cedar covered porch commonly called Solomon's Colonnade to teach those who came to the temple for the prayers and daily sacrifices. The Jewish leaders had once tried to seize Jesus there, but because of the crowd he had escaped and had gone to stay beyond the Jordan

---

1. 2 Timothy 1:7.
2. Matthew 10:16–31; Mark 13:11; Luke 12:11; Philippians 4:6–7.

for a while. While the apostles were teaching, the temple guards stormed in, arrested them, and took them to the prison for trial the next day.

"Brother, does this feel familiar?" Andrew said to Peter, trying to make light of the situation and trying to hide his own anxiety.

"In one sense, yes," but Peter was not thinking about his present discomfort. He was thinking of Perpetua, and of what Mary had said about the sword that pierced her heart. Would she worry about him . . . again?

Sensing his brother's concern, Andrew said, "Perpetua is in his hands too, brother. The promise is for her as well for as others. She is not alone tonight."

"Yes. Yes, I know that with my mind, brother . . . but my heart . . ."

"Peter, do you remember those nights when we were out on the Sea of Galilee? Those stormy nights when we fought against the wind and the waves for our very lives? How is tonight different from those nights?"

"My mind was not idle then . . . I was too busy thinking of survival. But now," Peter sighed. Where was his faith? Did he have enough faith for Perpetua too? "You are right. I must entrust her to the same one who is with us here in this prison."

They sat in silence for a while. They listened to the voices of the night guards as they relieved those of the day. There were still a few who were protesting their arrest, but they were told in no uncertain terms to go home. The sounds of the city at night began to filter through the high windows.

"Do you ever miss those days? I mean the time when we were still carefree fishermen."

"Carefree? Were we ever carefree?" Peter laughed. "But yes, I sometimes dream of being on the boat . . . we do have such good memories, Andrew. At times, I remember teaching you as a little boy, how to cast the net . . ."

"I remember falling in the water along with the net . . . how old was I? Five? Six? I was terrified! I thought the fish were going to eat me."

Peter laughed, "Yes, I remember that, but, to be fair, it only happened once. It didn't take you long to learn . . . fishing is in your blood."

"And now we fish for people."

"Yes, and you are good at that too." Peter suddenly turned to face his brother, "Andrew, I don't say this as often as I should, but I want you to know that I am very proud of you. I consider myself blessed to be your brother. Perpetua and I love you dearly."

"I know, brother," Andrew said, slightly taken aback by Peter's sudden sentimentality. "But I would not be here if it weren't for you . . . if you both did not believe in me and take care of me and invest so much of your lives in me."

"We have had some wonderful times together, no?"

"Yes, we have. I have wonderful memories . . . more than most men my age."

"And then our lives began again when you brought Jesus into my life," Peter said wistfully. "If it wasn't for your persistence, I might never have met him."

"You were rather sceptical back then . . . but for good reason."

"Andrew, truly, my only concern was for your safety."

"I know, I know. Thank you."

"But you were not alone in your pugnacity. Jesus was every bit as persistent as you were," Peter said, smiling. "He pursued me with a passion . . . he just would not give up."

"Like you when you were fishing. You never gave up until you caught something."

"True . . . and I suppose that is why we are here in this prison tonight."

"We won't give up."

"No. And we can't. We know the truth. No one can ever give up on the truth. A lie is easy to let go . . . but when you have seen what we have seen, heard what we have heard . . . you cannot let it go. You must share it . . . you must tell others . . . you must tell your children . . ."

"You must tell the world," Andrew filled in.

"Yes. We must tell the world. You know, I have often wondered how that will be . . . how will we tell the world, I mean? The Scriptures tell us the world will come to Zion[3] . . . are we to wait here for them to come?"

"Jesus said we would be witnesses to the ends of the earth . . . I think that means we will go to them. We are to do what Adam and Eve were meant to do . . . bring the world under his rule . . . but they stayed in the Garden."

"Yes, I understand that, but what of the Scriptures? The nations are meant to come to Jerusalem . . . to the city of the great king."[4]

"You forget that we – the community of Jesus – we are Zion now. We are the living stones of the New Jerusalem, as you have said yourself, we are the new temple.[5] Like the vision of God's moving throne in the scroll of Ezekiel.[6] He is with us now, remember? He is in us. Wherever we go, he is there. Wherever we go, we must make him known. So, in that sense, the nations *do* come to Zion when they come to him through us."

---

3. Isaiah 2:3; Micah 4:1–2.

4. cf. Psalm 86:9; Isaiah 2:3; Zechariah 8:22; Micah 4:2.

5. Hebrews 12:22; 1 Peter 2:5.

6. Ezekiel 1.

Peter frowned, "So, you are saying that by our going out into the world . . . by us making disciples of all the nations . . . we are bringing the world into the heavenly Jerusalem?"

"Exactly! Remember Jesus said that if we had faith the size of a mustard seed, we would be able to say to this mountain – and as I recall, he was looking at Mount Zion at the time – we would say to this mountain, 'be uprooted and cast into the sea.'[7] Remember him saying that? Well, we are that mountain and we will be cast into the sea of Gentiles . . . or at least that is how I see it."

Peter was silent for a moment, marvelling at how easily Andrew seemed to piece things together. "And that is how he is always with us . . . even to the end of the age," he mumbled, as if to himself.

"So . . . he is here with us *and* he is at the home of Mary with Perpetua."

Peter felt a hot tear roll down his cheek. Of all men, surely, he was the most fortunate. To have a devoted wife, a caring brother, supportive friends, and an ever-present Lord . . . for what more could he ask?

Suddenly he became aware of a warm presence behind him. He felt the hair on his neck rise as if someone was staring at him. He turned, fully expecting to see a guard or perhaps another prisoner . . . but the man behind him was no ordinary man . . . there was a light radiating from the being's face.

"Peter," the being said. Somehow, he knew it was an angel from the Lord.

"Yes, here I am." Peter marvelled at how calm he felt before this awe-inspiring heavenly being.

"Come. Follow me . . . you and all the apostles."

Peter stood and helped Andrew to his feet, motioning to the others to do the same. They followed the being through open gates . . . gates that had been shut earlier . . . no one stopped them or hindered their progress.

When they were outside the prison, the angel turned to them, "You must go to the temple and teach the people about the new life in Jesus." And with that he was gone.

The apostles were breathing heavily. What had just happened? Were they dreaming?

"I must first go to Perpetua," Peter said, "and we need to tell the others. But let us hurry as the night is far spent."

They hurried through the narrow streets, trying their best to be as quiet as possible. Rhoda was sleeping at the gate when they knocked. The poor girl had

7. Mark 11:22–23.

been waiting for their return. There was much joy and relief in the household as they were reunited with the other brethren.

"I knew the Lord was with me this time," Perpetua said to Peter. "I was filled with peace . . . a peace that transcends all comprehension. He truly is a comforter, this Holy Spirit . . . one who brings truth to calm my troubled mind,"[8] she said smiling, cupping his face in her hands. "You need no longer worry about me. He is with me as he is with you."

"This is what he told us would happen, Perpetua . . . he said we would be arrested and brought before councils . . ."

"I know . . ." she whispered softly in his ear. "As I said, I am at peace. Truly. Go now . . . you want to be there when the people arrive for the morning sacrifice. I am with you in spirit."

"I love you, my dear wife."

"And I you," she replied. "Be of good courage, preach the word . . . so many have not yet heard."

"I will." Peter walked away and then turned, "I will be back," he said.

"Go. Be blessed and be a blessing."

* * *

The sun was about to crest the hill when they entered the temple courts. A few priests were there, receiving the animals for the sacrifice. Some devout men and women began to arrive, and the apostles wasted no time in speaking to them about he who was the one and final sacrifice.

An eager crowd gathered around them as they taught the people about Jesus . . . what he had said and done, and how he had fulfilled the words of the prophets through his life and his death . . . how God had vindicated him by raising him from the dead,[9] and how he now had all authority in both heaven and earth,[10] seated, as he was, at the right hand of God.[11] Many had heard Jesus speak . . . many had seen his works . . . and they knew what had happened that fateful Passover. They had also heard about the wonders done by his followers, some even knew Asher personally and had heard him tell of his miraculous healing on several occasions. For that reason, many responded positively to the message of the apostles.

---

8. John 14:26.

9. 1 Timothy 3:16; Romans 1:4.

10. Matthew 28:18.

11. Luke 22:69; Ephesians 1:20; 2:6; Colossians 3:1; Revelation 20:11.

While they were still speaking, they saw the captain and his guards enter the court. At first, the guards did nothing as they feared the crowd. They did not wish to be the cause of a riot. The captain walked up to Peter and softly said, "Please. I am only doing my duty. Please come with us . . . now."

Some in the crowd were already beginning to protest, but Peter indicated that they ought to be at peace. He then motioned to the other apostles and they followed the captain and his men.

"How?" The captain said into Peter's ear.

"How, what?"

"How did you all manage to get out of the prison? The doors and gates were all securely locked this morning . . . the guards were all at their posts . . . but you were not inside."

"An angel sent from God released us and told us to go speak to the worshippers at the temple."

"An angel . . ." the captain was trembling, and beads of sweat were forming on his upper lip.

"Yes, an angel from God. I was every bit as surprised as you are now . . . but God will not be thwarted. He has told us we are to be witnesses and that he will not leave us."

"I must know . . . but I can't speak to you now. May I . . . later?"

"Yes," Peter said. "I am sure you will be able to find me."

The captain smiled, he already felt a sense of relief, "Forgive me, but I must do what I have been told to do."

"And we must do what we have been told to do . . . so, yes, I understand. There is nothing to forgive. Only believe and you will find peace for your soul. There is forgiveness with God in Jesus."

The captain said nothing more. The apostles were led into the room to stand before the Sanhedrin.

The high priest rose to speak. It was clear to the apostles that he was struggling to maintain his composure. He spoke slowly, but clearly, "I am not accustomed to being disobeyed," he said. Then, turning to John, he hissed, "And you! You who are known to our family. You are a disgrace . . . you are such a disappointment to us." He paused and breathed in deeply. He closed his eyes as if to collect his thoughts. He opened them and glared at Peter, "You were strictly ordered never to teach in this name again! Yet you have filled this city of Jerusalem with your instruction . . . and you are determined to lay the blame for this man's death at our door! You want to bring blood guilt upon us!"

Peter felt the familiar flood of calm sweep over him. The Holy Spirit was with him . . . there was no cause for fear or panic. He looked up and met the high priest's stony glare with determined compassion. "What we answered then, we answer still today. We must obey God rather than humans."

"The God of our Fathers," John interrupted, "raised Jesus from the dead . . . Jesus the man you had murdered by having him hung on a tree."

"As he said when he stood before you," Peter continued, "as he stood before you all . . . he said you would experience first-hand his exaltation to the right hand of God."[12]

He wanted them to remember the words Jesus spoke that night, words taken from the prophecy of Daniel[13] . . . words that the high priest understood only too well . . . words that brought the trial to its climax.

After a short pause, Peter continued, "God has indeed exalted this Jesus to be both the one true leader of Israel and the one and only saviour of Israel . . . the leader and saviour who was lifted up to grant repentance and forgiveness of sins to our people Israel."

"We are all witnesses to this reality," James added boldly.

"And so is the Holy Spirit," Andrew said, "whom God has poured out on those who believe in him and obey him."

"Enough!" the high priest roared, having finally lost the battle for control over his temper.

Someone cried out, "They speak blasphemy!"

"They are deserving of death!" others shouted.

"Brothers!" a voice boomed over the uproar, "Brothers! You forget yourselves!" It was Gamaliel, a revered and honoured Jewish teacher. The others fell silent. "Get them out!" he said to the captain. The apostles were ushered out once more.

"He will persuade them to be moderate in their judgement," the captain said under his breath. "He is the grandson of Hillel."

"Yes," Peter replied, "but be careful. There are eyes and ears everywhere. We can speak later when you are free."

"Why will they not be persuaded?" Philip asked the others. "They know that there is no body in the tomb."

"But remember," Thomas said, recalling his own doubts only too well, "Jesus said they would not be persuaded even if someone was to rise from the dead."[14]

---

12. Matthew 26:64; Mark 16:19; Luke 22:69.
13. Daniel 7:13; Revelation 1:7.
14. Luke 16:31.

"And," John added, "keep in mind that they cannot be persuaded without giving up everything they are . . . everything they live for . . . I know how they think."

"I do hope that they will not quench the work of the Holy Spirit . . . he will work in their hearts as he has in the hearts of so many others," James added.

"We must pray for them," Andrew said. "We must pray for them and all our leaders."

"O sovereign ruler of the universe," Peter prayed, "you alone can turn the hearts of leaders, whichever way you will.[15] You opened the eyes of the blind . . . open these spiritually blind eyes now. You unstopped the ears of the deaf . . . unstop the ears of these leaders. You are the light of the world . . . shine in us and through us, so that the darkness in the lives of these unbelieving men might be expelled. May all come to a saving knowledge of your Son, Jesus our Lord. Amen."

The others added their own prayers as they waited.

"You must return," the captain said.

"So soon?" Andrew said.

Once more they stood before the same body of men that had tried the Lord Jesus, knowing full well that they possessed the power to make good on their threats.

"You will be flogged for your insolence," the high priest thundered. "And you will no longer speak in this name . . . the name of this Nazarene!" Each word was weighed and measured and emphasized. "Have I made myself clear?"

Peter opened his mouth to speak, but the high priest clapped his hands together and shouted at the guard, "You! Get them out of my sight!"

The guards hustled the apostles into the yard behind the prison where they were stripped for flogging. Not all the guards were sympathetic, and especially the younger men tended to be sadistic, but the penalty was strictly limited to thirty-nine lashes each.[16] As they whipped the apostles, Peter began to sing the hymn they had sung during their previous incarceration. The others joined in enthusiastically, and soon they heard voices singing from the other side of the wall. The spirit of rejoicing numbed the pain, and soon the guards lost their lust for blood.

"Later," the captain said under his breath as Peter walked past him.

"Yes, later," Peter said without looking up.

---

15. Proverbs 21:1.
16. Deuteronomy 25:3.

They walked home, still praising and thanking God that they had been counted worthy of suffering for the name of Jesus. Some of the people followed them and joined in with their worship that day . . . that day and every day after, in the temple courts and in the various homes where believers met to learn more about Jesus. The apostles obeyed God and taught the people without further harassment. The captain became a regular attendee and began to learn how to be a witness to his colleagues and to the guards under him.

* * *

6

Priorities

"What is the fuss about?" Peter asked his wife as she met him at the entrance to the compound.

"The Grecian Jews are accusing the Hebraic Jews of not distributing the daily provision of food equally. They say they are neglecting their widows," Perpetua replied. "It is rather serious. There appears to be a misunderstanding, and the perceived language barrier has not made things easier. Mark has been helping with the translation, but there seems to be an underlying cultural tension as well."

"We have been so busy the past few weeks . . . what with the preaching and teaching . . . not to mention the imprisonments that took up a lot of our time."

Perpetua took Peter's face in her hands and looked into his eyes, "You cannot be everything to everyone, Peter. Perhaps it is time for you and the rest of the leadership to delegate some of your responsibilities to others. Even Moses had to appoint assistants to help him with the people."[1]

Peter pulled away slowly and sighed, "Perpetua, the need is so great. John tells me there are priests in the city who are starving.[2] Starving! I didn't want to believe it . . . and then I met a few who have joined our community, and they confirmed what John had said. Clearly, the leaders are not fulfilling the requirements of the law. The priests,[3] the widows, the orphans[4] . . . the law tells us clearly, they must be cared for. Someone must take up the responsibility for the poor . . . remember what Jesus said about inviting the poor and destitute to our banquets, giving a cup of cold water."

---

1. Exodus 18; Numbers 11.
2. Josephus, *Antiquities*, 20.181.
3. 2 Chronicles 31:4–10.
4. Deuteronomy 14:28–29.

"Yes, but you cannot fulfil all these things on your own . . . not even with the twelve and those of us who assist you. We now number in the thousands, dear husband, because of your preaching and teaching . . . and the miracles you do in Jesus's name."

"And because of our tangible love . . . don't forget, our message has a very practical side to it as well. We practice what we preach. It is by our love that people know that we are followers of Jesus."

Perpetua sighed. "My dearest husband, all I am trying to say is that you need to appoint others to help you achieve the things you are already doing . . . you need to delegate."

"I know, I know . . . you are right." Peter paused and then said, "I think I know what needs to be done. First, we need a few of the younger men to take messages to the others. I want us to assemble within the hour on the Mount of Olives, where we used to meet with Jesus. Then they need to choose able and mature representatives of each community so that we can discuss this and decide on some workable solution."

Perpetua lovingly touched her husband's cheek, "Thank you for doing this, Peter. I think you will see the wisdom of such a decision in the near future. Now, I will ask Mark and perhaps Andrew to help get the message out to them . . . you go and rest for a while. You are tired and weary, and that always makes you dark and moody, so go."

"What would I do without you?"

"Go . . ."

* * *

"But Peter, we simply cannot preach and teach and then also distribute food to the needy . . . if we try to do both, we will end up neglecting one for the other. We need time to read and study and discuss the Scriptures and you know how difficult that is, given the behaviour of some of the rulers of the synagogues."

"Brethren . . . please," Peter began raising his hands to quieten the group. "That is why I have asked for us to meet. You are right. We cannot neglect our regular times of prayer, nor our regular study of the Scriptures. So, like Moses of old, we need to delegate . . . we need to delegate responsibility to others who can perform the tasks we cannot get to on our behalf. Our community has grown to such an extent, that we have not been able to maintain our practical standards with regard to taking care of the needy, whether they are members of our group or not. So, while we apostles continue to do what Jesus told us to do, we will extend the authority he gave us to others . . . and it would be good if we could pass it on to others of the next generation, or even to those from a different background to ours . . . like the Grecian Jews, for instance. This way we will multiply ourselves in others."

James, the Lord's brother, indicated that he wished to address the group. His influence had increased in the past few weeks, and Peter noticed that many of the followers now sought his guidance. Peter thought that this was good.

"Brethren, Peter is right," James said. "I wish to propose that we select seven men . . . one for each of our congregations in the city . . . men who have a good reputation among us and among the people in general . . . men who are mature in their faith, who are filled with the Holy Spirit, who possess spiritual authority, and who have exhibited organizational abilities."[5]

There was a murmur among the disciples as they discussed what had been proposed. It was not a novel idea . . . Jethro had instructed Moses to appoint men to help him deal with the people of Israel in the wilderness.[6] Moses had later appointed additional elders.[7] This was nothing new, and it made perfect sense.

A Greek speaking believer spoke first, "I would like to propose Stephen to represent our community."

"We all know Stephen," Andrew said, enthusiastically, "he is a man of great faith and is filled with the Holy Spirit."

Another man spoke up, "And we propose Philip."

"Philip has already proved himself to be a great evangelist," Matthew said. "He is a good choice."

Soon, they had seven names, each man's character guaranteed by the testimony of the group as a whole.

"Do you men accept this role?" Peter asked. "If so, please step forward." Turning to the apostles he said, "I want to suggest that we lay our hands on them like Moses and the people laid hands on the priests when they commissioned them to be their representatives."[8]

"And like Moses laid hands on Joshua to be the leader of the next generation[9] . . . just as you said, Peter," Thomas added.

"Stephen, Philip, Procorus, Nicanor, Timon, Parmenas, and . . . Nicolas. Nicolas, am I right when I say you were not born a Jew but converted to Judaism?" Peter asked.

---

5. Exodus 18:21.
6. Exodus 18:24–26.
7. Deuteronomy 1:9–18.
8. Numbers 8:10.
9. Numbers 27:18.

"That is correct," Nicolas replied, looking a little worried. "Is that a problem?"

"To the contrary," John said. "The promise is not only for us and for our children, but for the world. In one sense, you represent the first fruits of that world."

Peter was so amazed that he couldn't think of anything to say. Was this the same John who wanted Jesus to send away the Syrophoenician woman? Who wanted to call down fire on a Samaritan village? Where was that racism now? How truly deep the work of the Holy Spirit was in his life.

"Shall we?" John asked, unaware that his statement had rendered his fellow apostle speechless.

"Yes," Peter replied.

They laid their hands on the seven, one at a time, prayed over them and commissioned them to do the work they had been chosen to do.

Later, when the apostles reflected on what they had done that day, they wondered that they had not done so much earlier. Because of the increased leadership, the community of Jesus flourished, and the word of God spread throughout the city. Many of the priests, seeing the love of the believers in action, became obedient followers of Jesus. Unity had been restored and, once again, the community could move forward to be what they were meant to be – the hands and the feet and the voice of Jesus . . . the body of the Lord on earth.

* * *

7

The Blood of the Martyrs

There was a soft, yet compelling knock at the door. Rhoda's face appeared in the crack.

"Yes, what is it, Rhoda?" Peter asked.

"Forgive me, Peter, but here is a man that says he was sent by Nicodemus. He says it is urgent."

The apostles looked at each other. Nicodemus was a member of the Sanhedrin. This could not be good.

"Send him in, please."

The young man came in the door. His eyes were wide and filled with fear.

"You have news, young man?"

"Yes. Stephen . . ."

Prior to joining the community of Jesus, Stephen had been a member of a synagogue known as the Synagogue of the Freedmen. The building boasted a large limestone slab with an inscription that indicated it had been founded by Theodatus, son of Vettenus, a priest who subsequently became the leader of the synagogue at that time. Theodotos was a descendant of a family of Jews taken to Rome after being enslaved by the Roman general Pompey many years earlier. They were later freed, and those who returned to Jerusalem started their own synagogue.[1] In addition to the synagogue, they had also built a small hostel

---

1. "A first century inscription, discovered by Raymond Weill in 1913–1914 in the lower City of David, confirmed the existence of a Greek-speaking synagogue in Jerusalem. The plaque identifies Theodotus son of Vettenus as a founder, priest and the head of the synagogue. The inscription credits the builder with the construction of ritual baths and a guesthouse available to travelers. Because Theodotus is a Greek name and Vettenus is a Latin name some scholars (Weill, Clermont-Geneau, Reinach, Vincent and others) theorized that Vettenus was a Freedman, who bore the name of his former master." Peter Shirokov, "Jerusalem Synagogue of the Freedmen (prof. Peter Shirokov, Eteacherbiblical)," Israel Institute of Biblical Studies, blog, 23 April 2014, https://blog.israelbiblicalstudies.com/jewish-studies/jerusalem-synagogue-freedmen-prof-peter-shirokov-eteacherbiblical/.

close by where Jews from abroad could stay while in Jerusalem.[2] Everyone thought it quite natural for Stephen to continue to attend their services and to evangelize his former friends and family who were still members. Their debates were often lively, but harmless.

"What about Stephen?" Andrew asked standing up, alarmed.

"A group of visiting diaspora Jews from North Africa, Cyrene and Alexandria to be precise, as well as a few from the provinces of Cilicia and Asia . . . most of them are temporary residents at the hostel . . ." the young man's voice faltered.

"Yes . . . spit it out, man! What is going on?"

"Well, a few days ago they began to turn hostile when they were unable to refute Stephen's assertions."

Stephen had been very well schooled and had memorized large portions of the holy Scriptures. He seemed to possess the ability to string together the minor narratives within the context of the larger narrative, and then come to a more comprehensive conclusion in the process. It was as if, in his mind, he looked down at the sweep of history from above, where he could view both the beginning and the end, as well as everything in between, and then sum it all up in a sentence or two.

"Nicodemus says," the young man continued, "that he thinks this group decided that the only way to get the better of Stephen was to twist his words . . . to make him appear to have said something he clearly had not . . . something inflammatory . . . something offensive to our leaders . . . some blasphemy about Moses, or the law, or the temple. It seems they convinced some locals to take a controversial matter addressed by Stephen out of context that could be used to accuse him of speaking out against God."

"Yes?" Peter urged. For a moment he remembered a similar frustrating conversation he had had with his brother years ago . . . Andrew too didn't seem able to get to the point.

"Well," the young man swallowed hard, "this wicked plan worked. Stephen was arrested and brought to trial before the Sanhedrin."

"What?" Thomas said, also jumping to his feet. "Where is he now?"

The young man hesitated, "They dragged him out of the city, and . . . and they have stoned him to death."

2. Carl Rasmussen, "A Jerusalem Synagogue Building from Jesus' Time?," HolyLandPhotos' Blog, 25 July 2016, https://holylandphotos.wordpress.com/2016/07/28/a-synagogue-building-from-jesus-time-in-jerusalem/.

"No!" All the apostles were now standing. "Why? Do you know what happened? Were you present at the trial?" Peter pressed him for more information.

"Yes. Yes, I was there."

"Well, tell us what happened," Philip nearly yelled out of exasperation.

"The witnesses came forward . . . they had been well prepared," the young man stammered. "Apparently, Stephen had said something to the effect that a day would come when Jerusalem and the temple would no longer be the centre of worship. But these men made it sound as if he had spoken out against everything our leaders hold sacred. Their testimony was damning . . ."

"Ah . . . the prophecy of Jesus about the destruction of Jerusalem,"[3] Andrew said almost under his breath. "He repeated the prophecy of Jesus."

"Please, continue," Matthew said.

"All this time, Stephen stood motionless before them. He appeared to be at peace . . . in fact, his face radiated serenity, and he looked, we all imagined, like an angel of God. I noticed the high priest shudder . . . I believe it was because of an unwelcome memory . . . we had seen this sort of composure before . . . in the face of Jesus . . . and in your faces when you stood before them too."

"You were at the trial of Jesus?" John asked. "But you are not a member of the Sanhedrin."

"No, I am merely a messenger. I am present at the gatherings, but only to run errands if need be."

"Please," Peter turned to look at the apostles, "let him finish."

"At this point, the high priest, Caiaphas asked for his defence. Stephen opened his eyes and fixed his gaze on each member of the Sanhedrin before proceeding. He urged them to pay close attention to what he had to say. Then he began to rehearse our history . . . the history of the Jewish people starting with Abraham." The young man had clearly been deeply moved by Stephen's speech. "But his genius in retelling these well-known stories was to expose the historic tendency of our people, especially the leaders of our people, to reject the emissaries of God. He brilliantly showed us how the patriarchs rejected Joseph and sold him into slavery, only to be humbled when God used him to rescue them from starvation during the famine. Then, moving on to the story of Moses, he revealed yet again how the appointed deliverer of Israel had been rejected at first and yet who, forty years later, turned out to be their liberator from slavery in Egypt. He went on to show how our forefathers repeatedly refused to obey him in the wilderness as well, in spite of the fact that they

---

3. Matthew 24:2; Luke 19:41–44.

had the very tabernacle of the testimony with them . . . they persisted in their tendency to worship the creation rather than the Creator."

The young man paused to catch his breath. Then he continued, "But the climax of his revision of our history as a people was to demonstrate that no tent or building could contain God, much less claim exclusive monopoly over his presence on earth. 'Is there a place that may serve as my dwelling?' he quoted from the Scriptures. 'For everything has been made by my hands.' Then he masterfully delivered his final, decisive blow . . . and this is what caused the Sanhedrin to lose complete control of themselves. To me, Stephen's voice sounded like thunder. 'How are you any different from our forefathers?' he shouted at us. 'You have all repeatedly resisted the Holy Spirit. Which of the prophets did your ancestors not persecute? They even killed those who prophesied about the coming of the righteous one. But you!' I noticed that his eyes were blazing with righteous indignation at this point. He looked at each member seated before him. 'You have committed a deed far worse than they ever did. You have betrayed and murdered the messiah himself!'"

The young man's voice broke. "Forgive me . . . it is all so terrible," he cried. "Suddenly, there was an uproar. A collective cry of fury rose from the members of the Sanhedrin. I've seen it so many times before . . . guilt manifesting itself in anger . . . and these men were no exception. They were like cornered animals . . . I could not believe the sudden transformation . . . they curled their lips and bared their teeth as they snarled at Stephen in uncontrolled rage."

The young man's sentences were coming out in short bursts between his sobs. Tears ran down his cheeks freely as he continued, "But in the midst of this disorder, Stephen suddenly raised his face and stared into a space beyond the room. 'Look!' he cried out. 'I see heaven opened. The Son of Man is standing at the right hand of God!' Those were familiar words to the members of the Sanhedrin, and they stabbed Caiaphas as if with a sharp dagger. You remember, John . . . you were there . . . Jesus quoted from the very same prophecy at his trial . . . indicating that, while they sat in judgement over him at that time, he would soon be revealed as the one seated in judgement over them.[4] And now Stephen . . . Stephen actually dared to state that this was a present reality. Well, that was the final stroke. Before he could regain his composure, Caiaphas and all the other members rushed at Stephen . . . they dragged him out of the city, and began to stone him, contrary, as you all know, to Roman law. There was no one there to stop them anyway. But they didn't care . . . they were wild . . . furious."

---

4. Matthew 26:64; Mark 14:62; Luke 22:69; Daniel 7:13; Psalm 110:1.

"Andrew, please get him some water," Peter said. "Go on."

The young man swallowed hard, "There was a young Pharisee . . . Saul is his name . . . the witnesses disrobed and left their clothes in his custody. There must have been about sixty or seventy men who surrounded Stephen . . . he was already wounded and bleeding because they had quite literally dragged him through the streets . . . kicking and hitting him as they went."

He grateful accepted the cup of water from Andrew and gulped down the contents, "Thank you." His hands were trembling. "The rocks they used . . . they were large enough to inflict damage, but not large enough to kill him outright. I think the object was to make his death as painful and as gruesome as possible. It was then that Nicodemus told me to run to you . . ."

Another knock on the door. Rhoda appeared once again. She was weeping and unable to speak. Three of the seven deacons pushed past her and entered the room. They were clearly distraught.

"Peter . . ." Philip began, "Stephen . . ." he was trying hard to catch his breath.

"We know," Peter said. "This young man is a messenger from Nicodemus. Were you there at the stoning?"

"We were all there," Timon said. "We could not get into the court room, but we were standing outside when they all came rushing out . . . they were pushing Stephen and hitting and kicking him . . . everyone was shouting and throwing dust in the air."

"We followed . . . but not closely," Nicanor added.

Andrew had fetched more water for the deacons. They slurped noisily between breaths.

"They dragged him out of the city," Philip continued. "It all happened so fast. The whole time I was wondering, where were the Roman guards? Why didn't they stop them? But there were none to be seen. The men were ripping off their outer garments . . . leaving them with this man at the gate."

"Saul," the messenger said, "it is the young Pharisee I told you about. He is a student of Gamaliel, but he is not at all like his teacher. He is not moderate in any sense . . . he is overly zealous for the law."

Was that a flutter of panic rising in his heart, Peter wondered. Jesus had spoken about persecution. Who was this young man, Saul? The messenger clearly did not like him . . . was he trying to warn them?

"Then they began to throw the stones at him," Timon said. "But even as the stones were hitting him, Stephen was praying for Jesus to receive his spirit. We were hiding out of sight, but we could see what was happening. We . . ." Timon shuddered as he relived the horror, "we watched as our beloved brother was systematically murdered by this bloodthirsty religious mob."

"Stephen finally collapsed and fell to his knees," Nicanor continued. "He was bleeding profusely, and his face was cruelly disfigured already . . . one of his eyes had been dislodged from its socket . . . his mouth was swollen, and a few teeth had been broken out. There was so much blood . . ."

The apostles winced as he painted the gruesome picture.

"But . . . but a look of love and compassion shone through the hideousness," Philip added. "Then we heard him cry out, 'Lord, do not hold this sin against them.'"

"The words of Jesus from the cross," John said. "Father forgive them . . . they do not know what they are doing."

"Yes . . . perhaps the leaders recalled those words of Jesus," Philip agreed, "but those very words proved to be too much for one of the men. He roared as he threw the final stone. It hit Stephen against his temple with such a force, that it broke open his skull. In that moment, he breathed his last breath on earth and drew his first in heaven."

For a moment there was silence. No one really knew what to say. They were struggling to process the shock and horror of it all.

The door burst open once more. The remaining two deacons and a few other young men carried in the blood-soaked body of Stephen, hastily wrapped in a large cloth.

"Get Perpetua," Peter said to Andrew. "Get all the women. Get water! Quickly!"

There was no time to waste. They needed to prepare his body for burial and get the word out as soon as possible. People had to be warned. It was no longer safe in the city of Jerusalem.

* * *

Part Two

"We will not withhold the [lessons from the past] from our children"

Psalm 78:4

8

The Seed of the Church

N o, Peter, I will not leave . . ."
"But Salome is leaving. You can go with her. Perpetua, please . . . Jerusalem is no longer safe."

"Salome is *returning* to her husband . . . not *leaving* him. No, Peter, my mind is made up. My place is at your side. Please, do not ask me to leave you. Like Ruth said . . . where you go, I go . . . where you stay, I stay."[1]

Peter sighed. He knew that once Perpetua was convinced about anything, there was no changing her will. And yet, the persecution was getting worse. The Pharisee named Saul was going from house to house looking for believers in Jesus, and if he found any there were no questions asked . . . he simply incarcerated them and gave them only one option. Renounce their faith in Jesus or face grim consequences.

Perpetua was well aware that she was complicating matters for her husband. But she had vowed to make her life with him . . . was that not what marriage was all about . . . to leave and to cleave . . . to never forsake the other, for any reason? Did the two not become one? How could she leave him in his hour of greatest need? To lead the fledgling community of Jesus through this time of trial would be difficult . . . very difficult. She needed to take as much responsibility off his shoulders as she could, even if it was merely feeding him and caring for his needs.

"Peter," she took his face in her hands and looked deep into his eyes. "Remember our wedding ceremony?"

"How could I forget? It was at once the most terrifying and yet most wonderful day of my life."

---

1. Ruth 1:16.

Perpetua smiled and gently kissed him, "That is true. I was very nervous and very, very shy. But Peter. The prayers our fathers spoke out over us . . . do you recall?"

"It is one of the prayers I have memorized . . . I was hoping to use it one day for our own children."

"Would you pray it . . . now . . . please?"

Peter cleared his throat. He closed his eyes, took her hands in his own, and recited from memory, "Blessed are you, Lord, God of our fathers, Ruler of the universe. Join these our children as you joined our ancestors in the garden of Eden, so that they may be made one, as our ancestors were made one. Blessed are you Lord, God of our fathers, Ruler of the universe, for you created woman for man so that he might not be alone. Unite this man and this woman so they may be husband and wife for life. Make them one for joy, for strength, for comfort, for love. Grant them life, peace, and happiness. May they live to see their children's children, and may you always keep them from the way of the stranger. Amen."

"Amen." She gently kissed both his hands and then looked back into his eyes once more, "There, see? Now, how could you ever ask me to leave you? I would be breaking my vows and throwing our fathers' prayer back in their faces."

"Perpetua . . ."

"No, Peter. My beloved is mine and I am his, remember?"[2]

"Perpetua, would you allow me to finish my sentence, please?"

"As long as you ask me to stay."

Peter sighed, "My dearest wife, I love you. I value you more than any other mortal. That is why I want you to go, but . . . shhh," he laid his finger on her lips as she attempted to interrupt, "I am speaking now . . . I want you to go, because I care for you, but"—It was his turn to take her face in his hands. He stared into her eyes . . . those deep, brown pools that sparkled like water in the sunlight—"But I know I need you here by my side as you fulfil me like no other. So, even though it scares me, it also calms me to know that you will be with me."

"And he will be here with us too . . . he promised to be with us always."

Peter nodded, "A threefold cord is not easily broken[3] . . . I only recently understood that verse, you know."

"A comforting verse . . ." Perpetua leaned in onto her husband's chest as he drew her to himself, "I feel so safe in your arms."

---

2. Song of Solomon 6:3.

3. Ecclesiastes 4:12.

"And I in yours . . . but the Father has his arms about us both."

"Then let us rest in his embrace . . . let us see where he leads us . . . in life or in death, we live for him."

"But in the meantime, we do need to make sure that the others are safe. They need to leave sooner, rather than later. There are temple guards and spies everywhere, so we will have to be creative."

"And we will continue to pray for the release of the others."

Peter lovingly kissed his wife gently on each cheek and then on her forehead, "I love you."

"And I you . . . now go and do what needs to be done. I will be here . . . waiting for you."

He slowly walked away but turned to look at his wife one more time before slipping through the door. He knew now that each parting might be the last . . . they must never take each other for granted . . . never again.

* * *

"It is because we neglected to move out from Jerusalem into Samaria and to the ends of the earth . . . that is why God has sent us persecution."

"How can you say such a thing, Thomas?" Peter was clearly shocked.

"Didn't Jesus tell us that we were to be witnesses in Jerusalem, Judea, Samaria, *and* to the ends of the earth?" Thomas stressed the "and" to make a point.

"Yes, but . . ."

"But what? We have been disobedient . . . and now we are paying the price."

"Thomas! Really! Our brothers and sisters are being tortured as we speak. To suggest that this is the will of our Lord is unkind . . . unkind to them and unkind to us. Jesus told us we would be persecuted. This is no punishment . . . this is the consequence of our preaching."

"Besides, the word *has* gone out to the ends of the earth," Philip added. "Many of those who were added to our community on the day of Pentecost took the message with them when they returned home. There are small communities getting together in many places . . . like the one in Damascus. I have heard reports about a certain disciple by the name of Ananias who holds regular meetings in his home."

"But it is *us*, Philip . . . we are the sent ones, remember? Jesus called us apostles. But I have not been sent anywhere. Since Pentecost, I have not been outside the walls of Jerusalem. You say the word has gone out to the ends of the earth, but there are people to the east of us who have never heard the truth. Alexander did not conquer the world by staying in Greece. And the

Romans . . . look at them now. Their empire is expanding because they keep moving outwards, further and further. They could have stayed in Italy, but they did not. We will not disciple the nations by staying in Jerusalem either."

"Thomas," the apostles all rose as Mary walked in. She had heard the discussion as she approached the room. "Thomas, do you not remember that Jesus said that they would do to us what they did to him? If they persecuted him, they will persecute those who follow him. It is the hatred of the truth that has brought upon us this horror. Since the day my son . . . since the day Jesus was born, he never punished anyone for tardiness . . . think back on the years you walked with him. He disciplined you, yes . . . he even corrected me at times when I clearly misunderstood his mission . . . but did he ever hurt anyone of you, or anyone else, for that matter?"

"Forgive me, Mary . . . I—"

"You are distraught," she interrupted, "I understand . . . like the rest of us. But this is not the time for disagreements and divisions . . . this is the time for us to be united and to stand together . . . to face this together. Remember, Jesus taught us that a divided kingdom will not stand. The enemy wants to divide us so that his servants might defeat us . . . we must not give him so much as a fingerhold in our midst."

"Forgive me . . . you are right," Thomas stammered. "I am distraught. On my way here, I witnessed the temple guards dragging a few of our brethren to the prison . . . but I could do nothing . . . I am so angry . . . I . . . I . . ."

"We have all seen things we could not have imagined, Thomas," Peter said putting his arm around his friend.

"We all hear the cries of those they torture," Andrew added.

"It is the times of silence that disturbs me most," John said. "These men can be so very cruel . . . but when there is silence, I wonder what they are doing to our brethren. How is it possible for anyone to be immune to such suffering? Have they no conscience or fear of God? I just don't understand how they can get pleasure out of brutalizing another human being."

A solemn silence filled the room for a moment.

Then James said, "But in one sense, Thomas *is* right. He is right in saying that we do need to be more mindful of the needs of those who were not represented here at Pentecost. Perhaps it is time for us to begin planning on taking the message of deliverance to those who are in total darkness."

"Yes," Peter said letting go of Thomas and sitting down. He was very aware of the heavy burden laid on his shoulders. How could he direct people to do that which might very well lead them into danger? "We need to seek the guidance of the Holy Spirit . . . he is the one who must lead us. It is not for us to make such decisions on our own."

"But we dare not move at present," Andrew began to say.

"And so we must spend our time in prayer and preparation," James added.

"But we must continue to teach our own disciples here . . . we must not neglect them," Peter reminded them. "We need to do with them what Jesus did with us. We must tell them what he did, what he taught us . . . we must train them, equip them . . . so that they may be enabled to do what we do. They need to know what we know so that they may do what we do. We need to duplicate ourselves . . . multiply ourselves."

"That's the first command ever given by God to humanity," Andrew said excitedly.

"I don't follow," Peter said, looking up at his brother.

"Don't you remember? After God created Adam and Eve, he told them to be fruitful and to multiply."

"Yes! Yes, that is right," Peter replied. "In many ways what Jesus commanded us to do is the same as what God told Adam and Eve to do . . . to be fruitful and multiply and to fill the earth . . . we are to make disciples of all the nations, even to the ends of the earth. But we must also remember that Jesus chose twelve of us out of the crowds . . . he taught them all, yes . . . but he took us and taught us more . . . he took us deeper."

"And out of the twelve, he went even deeper with you three," Andrew said, pointing at John, James, and Peter.

"True, but he expected us to tell you what we had seen and heard . . . what we had learned," James added.

"So, what are we saying?" Peter asked.

Again silence descended on the group as they thought about what they had just discussed. Then Andrew said, "I think – if I may sum up what everyone has said – what everyone is saying is that yes, we must get the word out to the ends of the earth . . . they would correspond with the crowds, in Jesus's case . . . but we are too few to reach them effectively . . . so we must reach them by equipping others to do what we do . . . to do the work of the ministry,[4] to spread the word, but also to do the other things necessary, like feed the poor and take care of the needy. If we can duplicate ourselves in others."

"I think that's what Jesus meant when he said we would do greater things than he did . . . he was only one person and could only be in one place at a time," James added.

---

4. Ephesians 4:11–13.

"But then he multiplied himself in us . . . in the twelve . . . and the women too," John said looking at Mary.

"And then after the resurrection, we were one hundred and twenty," Andrew added.

"And now . . . now the word has gone out to so many places through the thousands we have discipled since Pentecost," Peter said.

"And continues to go out through those scattered because of this persecution . . ." Thomas said. "I think I am beginning to understand."

"And that is why we cannot neglect to teach and to train our disciples really well . . . to make them copies of us as we are copies of Jesus . . . in this case, less is more," Peter concluded.

"Peter," Matthew interjected, "in the light of everything we have spoken about, I believe we need to write down what we learned. If this persecution has taught me anything, it is that our lives hang in the balance every day. If we do not commit to writing what we know, it may all be lost for posterity. We may not be alive to teach anyone . . ."

"I have been writing everything Peter teaches us." Everyone turned to see who was speaking.[5]

"Mark!" Peter smiled. "Come inside . . . don't stand there in the doorway."

"I . . . I did not wish to intrude," Mark stammered, "but mother sent me to call you for refreshments."

"A faithful messenger and a faithful scribe!" Matthew said, ruffling his hair.

"Please . . . don't . . ." Mark pleaded, retreating.

"Have you been taking notes?" Peter enquired.

"Yes, and I have been copying them out at night . . . they are not very neat . . . I scribble. And I don't think the stories are in the proper order either."[6]

---

5. According to Papias Mark "became Peter's interpreter and wrote down accurately, but not in order, all that he remembered of the things said and done by the Lord." In Eusebius, *Ecclesiastical History* 3, 39:15. See also Eusebius *Ecclesiastical History* 6, 25:5 where Eusebius quotes from a tradition received by Origen. There is a lot of speculation as to what is meant by "interpreter" and as to when and where Mark began to write. I believe that there is no reason to discount the fact that Mark was already one of Peter's disciples in Jerusalem prior to their missionary movements to Rome and elsewhere. Lane argues for Rome as do most scholars. See Marxsen, *Der Evangelist Markus*, 54–95 for his argument that Mark originated in Galilee. It is probable that the Gospel was compiled over time and likely that it could have been written in one place but copied and circulated in many others.

6. Moss ("Fashioning Mark," 196) summarizes a theory from Matthew Larsen's book, *Gospels Before the Book*. "Larsen argues that for early Christian readers, Mark's text was not a polished book but rather something more akin to υπομνηματα (notes) or απομνημονευματα (memoirs), terms that, in modern literary taxonomies, we might equate to something like a 'rough draft.'"

"But that is a wonderful start!" Matthew said. "May I see your notes?"

"Of course . . . but they are Peter's sermons and lectures."

"Peter?" Matthew looked at him enquiringly, "may I?"

"Of course . . . but I think we all need to sit down and discuss what each one of us can remember," Peter said.

"So that we don't leave anything important unwritten," John added.

"Exactly," Matthew said.

"I could tell you all about what happened before and after his conception," Mary offered, "but I think our kind hostess is waiting for us. Shall we?"

The apostles made their way to the door. Mary had started serving them in the courtyard since they were using the upper room for their meetings.

"I didn't know you were writing down my sermons," Peter said coming alongside Mark.

"Are you angry?"

"Angry? No! On the contrary . . . I only wish that others had been as industrious. You thought about doing something we have only begun to discuss now. Your notes will be very helpful to others . . . if you don't mind sharing them?"

"I'd be honoured . . . but I do want them back."

Peter was about to ruffle his hair, but then remembered that the young man did not appreciate it, so he resisted.

"Thank you for not ruffling my hair," Mark said, smiling.

"Unfortunately, you have very ruffleable hair."

They both laughed.

∗ ∗ ∗

9

Sprouting Seeds in Samaria

Yes?" Peter looked up at Rhoda standing in the doorway.

"There is a young man here who says he has a message for you," Rhoda replied.

"Oh . . . please, show him in."

A young man stood just in front of the threshold. He had long, curly hair, a bushy beard, and was of a lighter complexion.

"I come from Samaria," the young man said, still standing at the door. "Philip sent me with a message for you."

"Please come inside. Pray tell me, what is your name?"

The man at first hesitated, but then entered the room, "My name is Amram."

"You are a Samaritan?"

"Yes."

Peter extended his hand in welcome and then embraced Amram, kissing him on both cheeks. The man seemed surprised.

"How is it you were able to enter Jerusalem?" Peter asked.

"No one suspects a Samaritan," he replied gravely. "They are too preoccupied with trying to avoid touching me."

"I see . . . I am so sorry . . . it is only because of Jesus that I am not quite as offensive," Peter said, slightly uncomfortable, "but you said you have a message."

"Yes, from Philip."

"Amram!" It was Andrew. The two men embraced. "It has been such a long time since I last saw you! What brings you to Jerusalem?"

"You know each other?" Peter asked his brother.

"Yes, we met on our first journey through Samaria . . . at Sychar . . . oh, yes, you were not with us that time. Amram was one of the first Samaritans in that village to believe that Jesus is the Messiah."

"That is true . . . but we have since learned so much more about Jesus than what we knew then, Philip has been teaching us."

"How is Jochebed? And your son . . . I can't remember his name."

"Uhm . . . Amram?" he said with a smile.

"Of course . . . forgive me . . . how stupid of me. Of course you named him after yourself."

"Actually, I named him after my father," Amram said laughing.

"That's confusing. But tell me, how are they? Are they well? And the rest of the village? And you have not answered my first question . . . what brings you to Jerusalem?"

"You have not given me an opportunity to explain!"

The three men laughed. Peter thought back on the many discussions he had had with his brother where he felt the same way as Amram. Andrew had rattled on at such a speed that Peter was not able to get in a word.

"Philip sent me."

"Oh. So that's where they went? How is he? How is his family?"

"He is . . . they are all very well. Doing great things . . . just like Jesus."

"Yes, he was a good evangelist here too."

"No, no . . . I mean . . . well, yes, he is a very good evangelist, but the signs . . . and the exorcisms. So many people have been delivered from demonic possession . . . so many have been healed. There is great joy in our city."

"That is wonderful news, indeed," Andrew said, excited. "Not so, brother?"

"Yes, and even a man by the name of Simon—" Amram continued.

"That is a good name," Peter interrupted chuckling.

Amram looked confused.

"That is my brother's name," Andrew said.

"But . . . you are called Peter, are you not?"

"Yes, I am called Peter now, but my parents named me Simon . . . Jesus gave me my new name."

"And naming my son Amram is confusing?"

They all laughed.

"But what about this man Simon. Who is he?" Andrew encouraged Amram to continue.

"He was a sorcerer. A descendant of the clan of the magi. He had a large following . . . people marvelled at his powers. But he too put his faith in Jesus and now he follows Philip everywhere."

"And what is the message Philip sent?" Peter asked.

"He has asked that you come as soon as possible. He has baptized many, he baptized me too, in the name of Jesus. But he said he wanted us to be filled with the Holy Spirit."

"He wants us to come to Samaria?"

"Yes."

"I will need to discuss this with the others tonight," Peter said. "You will stay the night?

"If you will have me."

"If I will . . . ? Dear brother! You will be our honoured guest!"

Amram smiled, "It is going to be difficult to get used to being accepted by Jews."

"Perhaps, at first," Andrew said, "but always remember, it took us nearly three years before we understood that the kingdom was open to all, regardless of ethnicity."

"Yes," Peter said, "and even now, a few of our newer brethren struggle to come to terms with this inclusion. But know this. You are as welcome here as Jesus himself."

"Thank you," Amram said, bowing his head.

"Come, allow me to introduce you to our host."

* * *

They quietly slipped out of Jerusalem just before the sun crested the Mount of Olives. It was the time of day when one could see shapes, but not discern features. Amram walked tightly in front of Peter and John to give the impression that they were all Samaritans. The ruse worked and soon they were on their way to Samaria. No one thought to greet them much less accost them or question them.

When they were sure they were out of danger, Peter asked Amram to tell him what Philip had taught the group so far.

"Initially he taught us about Jesus being the ultimate sacrifice for sin," Amram replied. "It was wonderful to learn about the writings and the prophets. As you know, we Samaritans have only ever read the five books of Moses. Many still believe that the Jews who returned from the Babylonian exile corrupted the text and that we alone preserved the original."

He nervously glanced at Peter to see his reaction but seeing none he continued.

"He showed us how the Scriptures were fulfilled by Jesus . . . especially his suffering and his resurrection. In one sense, it was not difficult for us to understand the need for a perfect sacrifice . . . I think we have always known that the blood of the sacrificial animals cannot remove sin . . . that they are just images.[1] I mean, even if the animals are spotless and without blemish, they still cannot be adequate substitutions for our sins, because they are not humans. And no human could ever die for another human, as we all have our own sin . . . we have all fallen away . . . we are all corrupt, as Philip showed us in the Psalms.[2] So, we understood the need for the virgin birth, the sinless life, the death of Jesus . . . as Philip told us, Jesus is the reality of which the Passover lamb was only a foreshadowing. He said John the Baptizer called him the Lamb of God who takes away the sins of the world . . . that was not difficult for us to understand."

"Yes, it does seem as if the Scriptures were written to prepare us for Jesus, doesn't it?" Peter said. "It is as if we needed to see human failure in terms of keeping the perfect, good, and holy law of God . . . the inadequacy of the sacrificial system . . . the inadequacy of the priesthood . . . in short, the failure of human effort to live as we were created to live . . . the failure of even the best of us, in order that we could see our need for God to do what he did through Jesus."

"Indeed," Amram agreed.

"What else did Philip teach you?" John asked, impressed with what they had already heard.

"Well, after we said we believed that Jesus died as a substitute for us . . . now keep in mind that we had already accepted that he was the Messiah."

"That is true . . . it wasn't a huge jump to make," John said.

"In one sense, yes . . . we had already accepted him in life . . . but what we had to do this time was to accept him in his death and resurrection. But Philip opened up the Scriptures in such a way that it all made perfect sense . . . and after we said we believed his message he said we ought to be baptized. So, in preparation for our baptism, he taught us that, unlike the ritual purification washings we all know so well, baptism into Jesus means more. He said that it indicates a change in us . . . a change of status. He used so many examples, starting with creation . . . how life was only possible once the dry land surfaced from out of the waters[3] . . . and how a renewed creation emerged from the flood waters in the time of Noah[4] . . . and how our ancestors moved from being slaves to the Egyptians to being a free nation under God by crossing

---

1. Hebrews 10:4–10.
2. Psalm 14:3; 53:3; Romans 3:10–12.
3. Genesis 1:9–13.
4. Genesis 8:13–19.

through the waters of the Red Sea.[5] Once not a people . . . now God's people. And Joshua—I almost left out the story of Joshua—how the promise of God made to Abraham concerning the land was fulfilled once they crossed over through the Jordan river."[6]

"It sounds as if he taught you all well," John said. "Philip is very thorough, and he knows a lot of the Scriptures by heart. He has laid a very solid foundation for you. That is good."

"Yes, I realize we are very fortunate . . . blessed. But there was so much more he revealed to us . . . from the prophets Ezekiel and Zechariah and others. He taught us for days."

"Did he tell you why you needed to be baptized into the name of Jesus?" Peter enquired.

"Yes," Amram replied, "he said that by being baptized into the name of Jesus we were identifying him as our new head . . . the new head of a renewing humanity. Philip explained that it was an identification with his sacrifice of himself, once offered for us . . . a baptism into his death. He said that as the consequence of sin is death,[7] so in baptism we die with Jesus . . . the penalty for sin is paid by him for us . . . in him we are reconciled to God and set free from the curse[8] . . . but also, we are raised to new life in him.[9] Just like the dry land at creation, we can now sustain life."

"Yes . . . that is all very good, but baptism into the name of Jesus is also very much like when you were circumcised," Peter added. "You became a full member of the covenant people of God."

"I do not understand," Amram said.

"What I mean is that having been baptized into Jesus, you have been symbolically circumcised with the circumcision of Jesus."[10]

"But we have been circumcised already . . . must we be circumcised again?"

"No . . . no I'm not talking about the circumcision performed by a priest on the eighth day. No, rather I am talking about that which circumcision represented. Through the death of Jesus on the cross, that which circumcision

---

5. Exodus 14:29–31; Isaiah 11:15–16; Hosea 2:23; Romans 9:25; 1 Corinthians 10:1–2; 1 Peter 2:10.

6. Joshua 1:1–11; 24:11–13.

7. cf. Romans 6:23.

8. Romans 6:3–11.

9. Ephesians 2:6; Colossians 3:1; Hebrews 13:20–21.

10. Colossians 2:11–15.

symbolized was fulfilled . . . the stripping away of the sinful flesh by the shedding of blood."[11]

Amram breathed a sigh of relief, "I understand what you mean . . . you are comparing circumcision with baptism as the two signs that indicate entrance into the covenant. By being baptized into the name of Jesus, we have expressed our faith in his sacrifice of himself on our behalf . . . we have died with him, risen with him, and now we live in him . . . under his lordship."

"That is correct, but what Peter is trying to emphasize," John added, "is that baptism into Jesus is more than the ritual washings or even the baptism of John . . . it is more than repentance and purification . . . it is a change in your spiritual standing. You have now moved from darkness to light. From Adam to Jesus. From death to life."

"Yes, I understand," Amram said thoughtfully. "So, according to your analogy, Peter, through baptism into Jesus, we have entered into a new covenant with God . . . just like when Abraham was circumcised, and when he circumcised Isaac and all the men in his household."

"That is correct," Peter said, "but you must remember that that physical circumcision was only an image . . . a symbol of what was to come . . . a sign fulfilled in the death and resurrection of Jesus. Sin was passed down from parent to child . . . from Adam, as the head of all humanity, on to us . . . but now in Jesus, sin has been stripped away through the shedding of his blood. That is why we need to be *in* Jesus . . . baptized *into* his name. As the new head of redeemed humanity, if we are in him, Jesus's righteousness is now accounted to us.[12] Through baptism, we enter into a new covenant by his death that atones for our sin. So, just as the promise was for Abraham and all his descendants, so now, too, the promise is for you, for your children, and for as many as the Lord our God will call to himself.[13] The covenant has not become narrower . . . it has, in fact, expanded."

"So we are now under a new headship . . . all of us who believe in Jesus and are baptized into his name, cease to be in Adam . . . we are now, in Jesus," John added. "We are all members of the new covenant sealed in his blood."

For a while, the trio walked in silence. Such a great salvation demanded deep and grateful contemplation. The path on which they were travelling wound its way steeply through a densely forested area, but as they crested the mountains they were rewarded with a spectacular view of the western sea.

---

11. cf. Colossians 2:11–12.

12. Romans 5:17, 19; 2 Corinthians 5:21; Philippians 3:9.

13. Acts 2:39.

They had walked this way many times before, but today somehow everything seemed fresh and new . . . as if they were seeing life through new eyes. Before they began their descent to the low, soft rolling limestone hills of the coastal plains below them, they stopped to take in the panoramic scene before them from the heights of the Judean mountains.

Amram suddenly turned to look at Peter and John in a way that indicated that there was something more on his mind. "May I ask you another question?" he asked.

"You may ask as many questions as you please, Amram," Peter said laying a hand on the young man's shoulder. "In fact, I hope you will never stop asking questions. Life is a journey and we will never know all there is to know. When we stop asking questions, we stop learning . . . we stop growing . . . in a certain sense, we stop living."

"I will try to remember that. God willing, I will never forget it."

"What is your question?" John asked.

"Philip also spoke about a Holy Spirit. That we need to receive him or that we need to be filled with him. Who is he?" Amram asked.

"The Holy Spirit is the Spirit of Jesus,"[14] John replied. "He is the one who both gives us new life in Jesus and who helps us to live out that new life."

Amram turned pale, "So, faith in Jesus . . . baptism into Jesus . . . is not enough? We are lacking something?"

"No, no, no . . . that's not what I'm saying. Actually, I'm not sure you can separate faith in Jesus from the work of the Holy Spirit," John replied. "I think they go together. In many ways, Jesus's work of salvation, through his death and resurrection, is applied to us through the work of the Holy Spirit."

"So, do we have salvation in Jesus, or not?" Amram asked, clearly confused.

"You do. If you have confessed faith in his sacrifice on your behalf on the cross . . . and if you believe that God raised him from the dead, you have salvation."[15]

"Then why do we need the Holy Spirit?"

"Do you remember in the Torah how the Spirit of God would direct Moses . . . empowering him to lead the people of Israel? And how at some point he needed help . . . and that the same Spirit came upon seventy elders, who were then all empowered to help Moses?[16] Do you remember that?"

Amram nodded but said nothing.

---

14. Romans 8:9; Galatians 4:6; 1 Peter 1:11.

15. Cf. Romans 10:9.

16. Numbers 11:16–30.

"Well, it is the same Spirit . . . the Holy Spirit . . . only now he comes on us all," John said. "It was the Holy Spirit that led Jesus . . . he empowered Jesus to do what he did . . . and it was the Holy Spirit who raised Jesus from the dead. Just as he filled Jesus, so now he fills all those who are in Jesus . . . to lead us, empower us."

"Then why did we not receive him when we believed the message of Philip?" Amram asked.

"I'm not sure I have a good answer for that question," John replied. "Peter?"

"I've been thinking about this ever since you first delivered Philip's message to me," Peter said. "My first reaction is to say that the Lord may do as he pleases. Clearly, he has not poured out the Spirit on you as he did on us at Pentecost . . . and that is his prerogative. However, it may be that for some or other reason, Jesus wants us, as his appointed apostles, to be present when he pours out his Spirit on you Samaritan believers. Plus we . . . that is, John and I . . . we represent the Jerusalem community, a community which you know is made up of Jewish believers. Perhaps it is because Jesus wants us all to be one . . . Jews and Samaritans . . . this way our unity is preserved. Our presence ensures that the age-old animosity between Jew and Samaritan does not raise its ugly head in our community. If the Holy Spirit comes on you by the laying on of our hands, no one can ever say there is no connection between us. Does that make sense?"

Amram suddenly turned and spontaneously embraced Peter. He was weeping and for a long while he could not speak. As a father would embrace a child, so Peter held the young man in his arms.

"Forgive me," Amram said finally releasing Peter. He wiped his wet face with his sleeve. "I was so overcome with joy . . . of being accepted . . . of being part of one community, rather than two. It would have been so sad for us if, in spite of our common faith in Jesus, there was simply a continuation of our separate histories, don't you think?"

"Yes, my beloved brother," Peter agreed, "that would have been very sad indeed. Jesus said we must all be one, just as he and the Father are one. In fact, on the night he was betrayed, he prayed for us . . . but"—at this point, Peter looked straight into Amram's eyes—"But he also prayed for all those who would believe in him through our witness . . . so that we might all be united in him. One flock with one shepherd."[17]

For a moment the three men stood in a huddle, simply revelling in the pleasure of being considered brothers in Jesus. For so many years, since the

---

17. John 17:20–26.

disastrous decision of Rehoboam, son of Solomon,[18] they had been divided. In Jesus, that separation was now no more.

"Come, we must continue on our journey," Peter said. "I would like to be there before sunset, if possible."

"Yes," Amram said, "thankfully it is not much further . . . if we walk fast, we should be there soon."

"How fast do you want us to walk?" Peter said, pretending to be concerned.

"Fast enough, but not too fast for older men . . ." Amram said, chuckling.

"Cheeky youth!" Peter said laughing as he picked up his pace.

* * *

Amram insisted that they stay at his home. He said it was what Jochebed, his wife, wanted.

"Please," Amram pointed at two stools in the courtyard. His wife brought a basin and a towel. While it was a common custom in both their cultures, there was something remarkably beautiful about his washing his newfound brother's feet that evening. It was usually the task of the lowliest household servant, but when performed by the head of the household, it took on a whole new meaning. It was a statement of humble solidarity.

Peter then repeated the action for Amram for the same reason . . . the pillar of the church was also making a statement. He was a leader among many and a servant among servants.

When Philip and his family arrived, the noise level increased considerably in the compound. The reunion was as sweet as it was joyful. The threat of persecution had created an awareness of what was really important in life . . . every moment was precious, and nothing was to be taken for granted. They broke bread together and sang a hymn. Then they prayed . . . for those in prison, for those who were in hiding, for those who were continuing to spread the word wherever they went, for each other and for their friends and families . . . but most of all, they prayed for those who were persecuting them.

* * *

The following morning, Peter and John met with the Samaritan believers. There were many who remembered John and they were thrilled to see him. Their joy was palpable.

---

18. 1 Kings 12.

"I bring you warm greetings from your fellow believers in Jerusalem," Peter said to the assembled group. "Amram has told us a lot about you . . . Philip has taught you well."

Peter saw the Samaritan woman Jesus had spoken to at the well in Sychar so many years ago, standing close by, to his right. She had been one of the first to believe that Jesus was the long-awaited Messiah and had told her fellow villagers to come and meet him. Since that time, she had made right with the many people she had wronged, and was living a celibate life now, looking after orphaned children. John had introduced him to her earlier that morning. Somehow, he had always thought she would be older than she was. Perhaps it was because she had had four husbands and had been living with a fifth that had made him think so. Or perhaps the joy of her salvation simply made her look younger.

"Our history has been a long and unhappy one," Peter continued. "First, we were separated as a nation after Rehoboam refused the reasonable requests of Jeroboam.[19] At that time, our one faith took different paths."[20] He was choosing his words carefully as he did not wish to sound critical or superior.

"Then we were both subject to defeat and deportation . . . the northern kingdom conquered by the Assyrians,[21] the southern kingdom by the Babylonians.[22] As you know, the Assyrians repopulated your land with many foreigners from other conquered nations . . ."[23] Peter hesitated. This was a very sensitive point.

"It is all right, Peter," Amram said, "we are well aware of our mixed ancestry."

"Thank you, my brother," Peter said, glad to have been spared saying as much himself. "These two factors were the main reasons why the Jews refused to have dealings with you Samaritans in the past. While in Babylon, the Jewish sages came to the conclusion that it was for lack of purity and obedience to the law that our forefathers had been taken into exile.[24] And so, on their return, they searched the genealogies to make sure that everyone claiming Jewish parentage could prove their claim.[25] Those who had married foreign women

---

19. 1 Kings 12:1–24; 2 Chronicles 10:1–11:4.
20. 1 Kings 12:25–33.
21. 2 Kings 17:1–23.
22. 2 Kings 24–25; 1 Chronicles 9:1; 2 Chronicles 36:5–23.
23. 2 Kings 17:24–40.
24. 2 Chronicles 36:15–21.
25. Ezra 2:1–63.

were compelled to put them away, along with their offspring.[26] The Torah was read and explained to them . . . and the leaders began to provide commentary on every law, in an attempt to ensure obedience.[27] Unfortunately, later many of the people did not know the difference between the written law and the oral law. To them they were just rules to obey and very few ever questioned the reasons why."

The crowd before him were listening intently. So far, he had not offended anyone.

"This was the beginning of the deep rift between us as returnees. You know the stories of the governor, Nehemiah and the scribe Ezra. I do not need to repeat that history, or do I?"

The people indicated that they understood and that he could continue.

"And the question as to where we were meant to worship . . . well that was a further wedge driven between us . . . a wedge, I believe Jesus addressed when he spoke to you many years ago. As you now know, the time has come – and it is now – when the worshippers of God will no longer worship at Mount Gerizim, or at Mount Zion. We now worship God in spirit and in truth.[28] In Jesus, geographical location and buildings built of stone are no longer relevant. We are being built into a holy community as living stones. Jesus is himself the chief cornerstone of this spiritual building.[29] Together, those of us who believe in Jesus, Jews and Samaritans, together we are the new restored Israel of God . . . we are the new royal priesthood . . . we are his own chosen and precious holy nation through whom God would make himself known to all peoples. We are no longer separate. In Jesus, we Jews and Samaritans, we are one."

The deafening praises mixed with copious tears took Peter by surprise. Someone began to clap their hands rhythmically and the crowd began to sing a hymn Philip had taught them. It was a while before Peter was able to continue his address.

"Before returning to heaven to be seated at the right hand of God the Father, Jesus told us that he would send us a gift from the Father . . . a gift that would empower us to be witnesses to him in Jerusalem, Judea . . . yes, and Samaria too . . . indeed to the very ends of the earth. I believe Philip has told you all about the Holy Spirit, yes?"

26. Ezra 9–10.
27. Nehemiah 8:1–9:36.
28. John 4:19–24.
29. 1 Peter 2:4–8.

The people nodded yes, their faces shone with excitement and eagerness. Philip had told them that Peter and John would be praying for them so that they, too, might receive the Holy Spirit.

"You have confessed faith in Jesus and believe that he died and rose to life. You have all been baptized into his name. All that remains is for you to receive the Holy Spirit, so that you may participate fully and equally in our mandate to make disciples of all nations. John and I are going to pray now for you as we prayed in the upper room before Pentecost . . . for God to fulfil his promise and to pour out upon you what was prophesied by the prophet Joel."

Together, in the same manner in which they had laid hands on Philip and the other deacons, Peter and John now laid their hands on the new believers. Each one received the promised Holy Spirit. There was much joy and great celebration that day.

* * *

"There is someone here to see you, Peter," Amram said. "His name is Simon. I believe I told you about him. He used to be a great magician and led many people astray . . . but he has said he now believes in Jesus. You prayed for him today. May I show him in?"

They had just finished a hearty meal served by Jochebed and a few other local women. Peter was tired. John had already gone to bed.

"Could this wait until morning?" Peter asked, hopefully.

"He says it is urgent," Amram persisted.

"I will go down to him," Peter said. "There is no need to disturb everyone at this hour."

Peter walked down to the courtyard where Simon was still standing. In the poor light of the oil lamps, the man looked smaller than Peter remembered. He had his hands folded one over the other and he moved them as if he was washing them in water. His shoulders were slightly hunched. But he was a handsome man and possessed a form of dignity. Peter could see why he could have had such influence on people . . . there was something regal about him.

"Simon, it is late . . ." Peter began.

"Yes, I understand," Simon replied, continuing to wash his hands in the air, "but I was wondering if I could purchase your abilities."

"If you could what?" Peter knew that to speak when he was tired was not a good idea. He was far too irritable and was liable to say something he would later regret.

"The price doesn't matter. I have enough gold and silver to pay whatever you require. But I do wish to have the same power you have . . . to have the ability to lay my hands on people so that they might receive the Holy Spirit."

Did this man just say he wanted to buy the power to give what only God could give? In his mind's eye, Peter saw Jesus driving the money-changers out of the temple with a whip.

"You think you can buy the gift of God with money?" Peter just barely managed to keep his voice down. "May you perish along with your riches! You will never have a share with us in this ministry, as your heart is wicked and not right with God."

Peter swallowed hard. He was trembling with righteous anger.

"My advice to you is that you repent of your wickedness immediately. Go! Pray to God that the deliberations of your heart might be forgiven you! You are filled with everything foul . . . bitterness and greed . . . and you are not free . . . you remain a slave to sin!"

Simon realized that he had underestimated Peter and he was filled with fear. Through his foolishness he had exposed his raw desire for power. But he felt no remorse. He was merely terrified of the consequences. Rather than pray to God himself, he asked Peter to pray for him so that what Peter had said would not come to pass. With a sinister hiss, he turned on his heels and fled the compound.

Peter sighed deeply. He needed to go find a pillow.

* * *

Peter and John stayed with Amram and Jochebed for another three days before returning to Jerusalem. During that time they took Peter to see the well purchased by Jacob at the foot of Mount Gerizim. It had a narrow opening, dug through limestone, and was quite deep. The walls around the opening were attractively constructed with finely cut and shaped stone. They hiked up Mount Gerizim to view the ruins of the temple destroyed by John Hyrcanus, one of the Hasmonean priest-kings, more than a hundred years ago. It was still an active worship site for the Samaritans, so they did not go too close lest their presence offend the people.

They taught the people more about Jesus, his ministry, and their role in the discipling of the nations. Those who were sick came for prayer, and the demon-possessed were brought for exorcism. But Philip had taught them well, and so, after three days, Peter felt they ought to go back home.

Rather than follow the same route home, they decided to tour many of the Samaritan villages in the south, to share the message of Jesus with them. Reaching out to the Samaritans was a priority, as Jesus had specifically mentioned Samaria in his final instruction. It was the beginning of the healing of the fracture between those who had once been relatives.

* * *

10

A Dry Branch Blossoms

I have a message for Peter from Philip," the messenger said.
"Please come in, brother," Peter waved the man in. "You are most welcome."

"And how is Philip and how is his ministry in Samaria?" John asked, handing the man a cup of water.

"Philip and his family are well . . . but I do not come from Samaria," the man replied, gulping down the water thirstily.

"Oh?" Peter sounded surprised, "Where are you from then?"

"I have come from Caesarea Maritima."

"Caesarea!" Peter exclaimed. "My, he does get around, this Philip."

"What is he doing in Caesarea?" John enquired.

"I think he explains everything in this letter," the messenger replied, handing over a piece of parchment to Peter.

Peter unrolled the small scroll, his eyes scanning the contents. For a moment, he said nothing.

"Well," Andrew said, "are you going to share the substance of the message with us?"

"Yes . . . yes, I'm sorry." Peter cleared his throat, "Philip writes: 'To Peter and the community of Jesus in Jerusalem. Grace and peace to you from God our Father and from our Lord Jesus Christ, through the power of the Holy Spirit. I am writing to you all from Caesarea, where we are based now.'"

"You can hear he has been schooled in the Greek methods . . . so formal," Matthew said.

Peter peered over the parchment at Matthew, but when he made no further comment, Peter grunted and continued to read, "'Recently, I have been meditating on the promises found in the scroll of the prophet Isaiah.

One reads: "Besides the outcasts of Israel, I will gather in still more."[1] Another promise states, "the eunuch who keeps my sabbath and chooses to do what pleases me, keeping my covenant, I will give a future in my house better than many sons and daughters and a name that shall never be cut off."[2] And also, "I will bring the foreigners to my sacred mountain and grant them access to my house of prayer." These promises and more concerning the marginalized and disenfranchised have been on my mind for some time now, and I have been praying for the Lord to show me how they could possibly be fulfilled."

"Marginalized and disenfranchised . . . what does that mean?" Thomas enquired.

"It means those who are excluded, those who are considered outcasts," Matthew offered.

Peter grunted again and continued reading, "'As you know, the Lord saw fit to bring into his kingdom our lost Samaritan brethren through my ministry to them. You came and prayed with them and they all received the Holy Spirit. The man named Simon, whom you know well, has moved away . . . some say he has relocated to Rome. But I digress. Shortly after you left, an angel of the Lord instructed me to travel south along the desert road towards Gaza.'"

"This sounds like the stories we read about Elijah or Elisha," Andrew interrupted.

"Indeed. Shall I continue?" Peter was surprised at his level of irritation. He had not yet recovered from their trip to Samaria and fear of being captured was their constant companion.

"Yes . . . forgive me, brother . . . I won't interrupt again."

"It's not a long letter . . . allow me to read through it and then we can all comment." Peter knew he was tired. He felt like he was carrying the world on his shoulders since the persecution broke out. Perpetua had warned him that he needed to get adequate sleep, but how could he sleep while Satan prowled about the city like a roaring lion?[3]

"Please continue," Matthew said.

"Where was I? Oh, yes. 'As I was walking, I saw what appeared to be a chariot transporting an important individual. At that moment, the Spirit prompted me to approach it, so I did without hesitation. Inside the chariot sat a handsome dark-skinned man with thick, black, curly hair. I assumed he was from Africa. As I walked alongside the chariot, I heard him reading aloud

---

1. Isaiah 56:8.
2. Isaiah 56:4–7.
3. 1 Peter 5:8.

with difficulty from the Hebrew scriptures, specifically from the scroll of the prophet Isaiah. Addressing him, I asked, "Are you able to understand what you are reading?" I think at first, I startled him as he was deeply absorbed in the reading. "No," he replied, "How can I, unless some person explains it to me?" He told me that he was a Eunuch – now you understand why I have been meditating on the previously mentioned verses – in the service of the Candace, the queen mother of the Ethiopians, and that he was a convert to the Jewish faith. She had given him leave to go up to Jerusalem to worship and while there he had acquired a copy of the scroll he was reading. He invited me to join him in his chariot, which I did. I then saw that the specific portion he was reading from was where Isaiah spoke about the suffering messiah being led like a lamb to the slaughter.[4] He was confused. Was the prophet speaking of himself or some other person, he enquired. Beginning with that passage, I told him all about Jesus, just as you instructed us. I believe I am correct in saying that this method of instruction was taught to you by Jesus himself. We travelled on for a while when suddenly the man indicated that he believed, and that he desired to be baptized in the name of Jesus. We were right alongside a brook in the Valley of Elah, where King David slew Goliath,[5] so I baptized him there. As he came up out of the water, he was filled with joy and praised God. But suddenly, and unexpectedly, the Spirit lifted me up and transported me to Azotus.'"

Andrew opened his mouth and then shut it again. Better to let his brother finish reading first.

But Peter had paused, silently rereading the last line to make sure he had read correctly. "Astounding," he said. "Philip continues: 'I do not know what has happened to the man, but I am certain his name is written in our Lord's house. It seems to me that the Lord is slowly leading us out further from the centre into the regions he spoke of just before he returned to heaven—'"

"That's just what I was saying ought to happen!" Thomas blurted out, "Only I want to go to the East . . . everyone else seems to be going West."

"Yes, Thomas," Peter sighed, "we really do need to start asking for the Holy Spirit's guidance. He is very obviously leading our brother, Philip. But let me finish . . . there's not much more. 'I am now here in Caesarea,' he writes, 'where I may stay, as the Lord has granted me an open door for ministry in the surrounding area. Pray that the Holy Spirit will break up the hard soil of

---

4. Isaiah 53:7–8.

5. See 1 Samuel 17. The biblical text does not say where the Eunuch was baptized, but this is a possible location.

the hearts of our fellow Jews, so that the seed we sow may fall in well-prepared soil and produce even more abundant fruit for his glory. The small community that meets in our house sends greetings. Walk with the Lord. Amen.'"

"Amen!" John shouted. "All praise and thanks be to God!"

Suddenly, the door to the room burst open. Mark stood in the doorway, breathless and wide-eyed.

"Saul . . ." he said breathing hard.

Peter stood up, alarmed.

"Saul, has obtained letters from the high priest . . ."

Andrew handed the young man a cup of water.

"Thank you." Mark gulped down the contents, and then continued, "Saul, has obtained letters from the high priest giving him authority to arrest anyone who believes in Jesus, not only here, but in Damascus as well."

"What?" James almost shouted.

"We must warn Ananias," Philip said.

* * *

11

The Wolf Lives with the Lambs

The wolf now lives with the lambs," Peter read out loud.

"What does that mean?" Andrew asked.

"I'm not sure," he replied, "but seeing that it comes from Ananias, it may be referring to Saul."

"Then why doesn't he say so?" Philip asked.

"Perhaps he is afraid his message will be intercepted," James offered.

"I still have connections in the family of the high priest," John said. "If it is about Saul, I am sure they will know what has happened."

"The wolf now lives with the lambs," Peter reread the message. "It is an allusion to the prophecy of Isaiah . . . about the time of the Messiah. Remember? Andrew?"

"Yes, it is from the passage that speaks about the shoot coming forth from the stump of Jesse. The wolf will live with the lamb, the leopard lie down with the kid, the fatted calf dwell with the predator, a young child shall lead them,[1] all the earth shall be covered with devotion to the Lord, even as the waters cover the sea,[2] the stock of Jesse will become the standard for all people.[3] It goes on to speak about the nations seeking his council[4] . . . I'd have to find a scroll and look again . . . but I am sure it speaks about people being redeemed from Assyria and Egypt and other lands . . . all coastlands."[5]

"If Saul is now one of us . . . then what is to stop us from taking the message of Jesus to all people?" Thomas was getting excited again. It seemed to Peter that he had a burden for the lands of the East.

---

1. Isaiah 11:6.
2. Isaiah 11:9.
3. Isaiah 11:10.
4. Isaiah 11:12.
5. Isaiah 11:11.

"See what you can find out, John," Peter said. "Once we are sure, we can talk again."

* * *

"It is true," John confirmed, "Saul has become a follower of Jesus."

"Thanks be to God!" Matthew cried.

"I was told that it happened while he was travelling on the road to Damascus," John continued. "They say he is delusional . . . he claims Jesus appeared to him on the road. Apparently, there was a bright light that struck him blind. Then he heard a voice from heaven asking, 'Saul, Saul, why are you persecuting me?' When he asked the voice to identify himself, the voice apparently claimed to be Jesus."

"Jesus!" Mary of Magdala exclaimed, "He identifies himself with us . . . to persecute us is to persecute him."

"What's more," John continued, "they say that after Saul was healed of his blindness by a man named Ananias, he *did* go to all the synagogues he had intended to visit . . . but not to arrest the followers of Jesus. Rather he went to tell those who did not believe in him that Jesus is the Son of God. Apparently, he stumped them with his proofs as I can well believe. Remember, he sat under the tutelage of the great Gamaliel . . . if anyone knows the Scriptures, it is him."

"So they know it was Ananias who healed him?" Peter asked, concerned.

"It seems so," John replied.

"So where is Saul now?"

"They are not certain. Some say they heard he went into seclusion somewhere in Arabia."

"Is he to be trusted?" James asked.

"I know Saul of Tarsus," Barnabas said, "he is not one to profess what he does not believe. He is too traditionally honest for that."

"Well, I do believe we need to take advantage of this lull in the persecution," Peter said. "A few days ago, I received a letter from a small group in Antioch, asking for me to come to them. I have discussed this at length with Perpetua and we decided that as soon as it was safe for us to travel, we would go. It seems, now is the time."

* * *

Part Three

" . . . all the peoples
of the earth will be
blessed through you"

Genesis 12:3

12

Widening Circles and the Ripple Effect

I bring greetings from our brethren in Antioch," Peter said.

There had been peace in the region ever since the strange news about Saul of Tarsus had reached them in Jerusalem. The former persecutor of the believers had apparently emerged out of his seclusion in Arabia and was disturbing the Jews greatly in Damascus, proving that Jesus is the Son of God.

"You two have been gone a long time, Peter and Perpetua," Mary said affectionately, "what, nearly three years, now? We have missed you both and have been praying for you daily."

"Thank you," Perpetua said reaching across the table to take Mary's hand in her own, "we were very aware of your prayers."

"Yes, thanks to your prayers," Peter added, "all has gone well on this trip."

"Indeed," Perpetua interrupted, "we had the most uneventful journey. We did pass a few Roman soldiers on the way, but they were there to protect us, not harm us. We felt very safe."

"Yes, and if there is one thing I can say for the Romans," Peter added, "they know how to build roads . . . and for that we are grateful, even if they only built them to ease the movements of their troops."

"To deal with scoundrels like us, do you mean?" Philip asked jokingly.

"Especially a scoundrel like you!" James said, poking him in the ribs.

They all laughed. Such a weight had been taken off their shoulders since the persecution had ceased.

"How are things in Antioch, brother?" Andrew asked.

"Good . . . in fact, very good. As you all know, some of our brethren here went to Phoenicia and Cyprus after our brother Stephen was murdered, and they preached in the synagogues there and persuaded a number of our countrymen to follow Jesus."

"Cyprus!" Barnabas said, his face brightening up. "My adopted home. I have heard such wonderful news from friends and family on the island."

"Yes, it is wonderful to see how these communities are flourishing," Peter said. "Do you all remember that woman in Phoenicia whose daughter was possessed with a demon?"[1]

"You saw her?" John asked, feeling a sense of guilt rising within. They had treated her shamefully, but the shame was theirs to bear in the end. Jesus had exposed their racist inclinations and had praised this Gentile woman for a faith they, as yet, had not attained.

"Yes, we saw her . . . and she introduced us to the community that meets regularly in her home. Her daughter has married a fine young man . . . a strong believer in Jesus."

"That is wonderful news," Andrew said.

"Yes, we were encouraged to see how the communities were thriving. But, to continue"—Peter cleared his throat—"at that same time, others went to Antioch. When we arrived, to be honest, we did not really know what to expect. Antioch is no small city. Some consider it to be the third largest in the Roman Empire, only Rome and Alexandria outrank it. There are so many huge pagan temples and Roman theatres and Roman baths . . . all so foreign to us. But we were thrilled to find that there are quite a few strong groups there that meet regularly from home to home, just as we did here in the beginning."

"How has the message of Jesus been received there?" Philip asked. "Have they met with any opposition from the synagogue leaders yet?"

"No . . . in fact they are well received and still attend the synagogues on a regular basis, telling them about Jesus."

There was a loud banging on the gate outside. Rhoda ran down to see who was there. They heard someone running up the stairs and then John Mark burst into the room.

"I have just heard that Saul is back in Jerusalem," he said, out of breath.

"Saul!" Thomas exclaimed. "The persecutor?"

"The same," Mark said, standing bent over with his hands on his knees, "I have been told he is looking for you, Peter."

The initial stunned silence was shattered when everyone began to speak at once. No one knew what to make of this news. All they knew was that Saul had apparently become a believer, but then he had gone into seclusion in Arabia.

1. Matthew 15:21–28.

There had been rumours that he had returned to Damascus, but what was he doing in Jerusalem? Emotions were running high.

"Quiet down . . . quiet down," Peter shouted above the din. "I understand your concern, but—"

"The man is a murderer," Procorus interrupted, "he is not to be trusted!"

"Not only that," Nicanor said, "it is like a nightmare has returned. I can still see his stony expression before my eyes, as if it were yesterday. This is the man who didn't even flinch when Stephen's eye popped out of its socket."

"Indeed!" Procorus added, "He is a monster . . . he approved of the stoning. All that blood . . . I can still hear Stephen's prayers in my dreams at night . . ."

"Can you? Can you really?" Barnabas interrupted. "Then you must remember what Stephen prayed for . . . he prayed for his murderers . . . he prayed for Saul . . . he prayed that they might be forgiven. Who are we then to withhold what he prayed for?"

"But Barnabas," Nicanor interjected, "what about those he captured through cunning and deception . . . how are we to know that this is not all a ploy to gain access to our community? How do we know he will not imprison us all once we are exposed?"

"I agree . . . just think about those he incarcerated!" Procurus asked, "Have we forgotten how he tortured them? Our women and our children? Nicanor's wife was one of them. How is one to trust a man like him?"

"Have you forgotten, Peter?" Nicanor said through clenched teeth, "Have you? My son still has sleepless nights . . . he still hears his mother's screams . . ."

"We must learn to put the past behind us," Peter pleaded.

"How? It is not that easy," Nicanor interrupted, shedding angry tears. "The past lives inside us. It haunts our nights and troubles our days . . . how can you say we must put it behind us as if it is an old worn-out garment? It is the clothing we wear under our skins."

"Nicanor, my brother . . . forgiveness is putting off the old worn-out garments," John said tenderly, putting his hand on Nicanor's shoulder. "It is putting them off and putting on new garments, the garments of forgiveness and reconciliation. We have to love even as Jesus loved, my brother[2] . . . he loved even to the point of death on the cross.[3] It is through his death on the cross

---

2. 1 John 3:16.

3. John 15:13.

that God demonstrated his love for us,[4] and we simply cannot say we love God if we are unable to love as he loves[5] . . . if we cannot love even our enemies."

"Jesus told us that we must love our enemies,"[6] Peter reminded them, "he prayed for the Father to forgive those who tortured him and murdered him."[7]

"Yes . . . yes, I know . . . and Stephen prayed the same," Procurus exclaimed, a little too loudly. "We know all that, Peter . . . but to do what he did, Saul has to have a heart of stone. Can a leopard change its spots, Peter? . . . Barnabas?"

"The Lord promised in the Scriptures that he would break up stony hearts,"[8] Andrew interjected. "He broke up our stony hearts and gave us hearts of flesh. Have you all forgotten that we too were once in need of forgiveness and inner change?"

"At one time, James and I were quite willing to turn our backs on the very Phoenician woman Peter spoke about . . . we were quite willing to allow the demon to continue tormenting her daughter . . . this pagan woman who now has a thriving community of believers in her home," John said in support of Andrew. "That, in itself, was a murderous act too."

"We were deaf to her cries for mercy too," James added, "just as Saul was deaf to the pleas of our brothers and sisters. We were no better than him."

A strained silence descended on the group.

Barnabas broke the quiet, "I will go meet with him."

Peter sighed, "Thank you, Barnabas. Bring him to me . . . I will talk with him."

"As will I," James, the brother of Jesus said, standing beside Peter.

"It might be wise to meet him elsewhere . . . other than here," Andrew whispered in his brother's ear. "The wounds are deep here, Peter, and still quite raw."

"We will meet him in the garden . . . where we used to go with Jesus," Peter said.

"Very well," Barnabas said, "I will meet you there soon."

* * *

"It is not safe for Saul to stay here," Peter told the group.

---

4. Romans 5:8.

5. 1 John 4:20.

6. Matthew 5:44.

7. Luke 23:34.

8. Ezekiel 36:26.

"Why?" James asked. "What has happened? I heard that things were going so well. That he was speaking fearlessly in the name of Jesus and even debating some of the Hellenistic Jews."

"That is the problem," John said. "We have heard rumours that they are plotting to kill him."

"Now the hunter has become the hunted," Nicanor said under his breath but loud enough to be heard.

"That is not helpful," Peter said, a little too sternly. "You must remember he is a brother in Jesus now . . . and it is our duty to protect our own."

"He must go back to his hometown," Barnabas said. "He will be safe there."

"We – that is Perpetua and I – can escort him as far as Caesarea. We have been planning to visit our brethren in Lydda."

"How soon can you leave?" Barnabas asked.

"We leave in the morning," Peter replied.

"I will make sure he is ready."

∗ ∗ ∗

"You think he will be all right, Peter?" Perpetua asked as they watched Saul sail away to Tarsus.

"The Lord will watch over him as he watches over us all. I believe that we have not heard or seen the last of Saul."

"Yes, I get that impression too . . . that the Lord will do great things through him one day."

"Then we will pray in that manner." Peter put his arm around his wife and drew her closer to himself, "I am so blessed . . . you are truly a perfect companion for me. You fulfil me in so many ways."

Perpetua smiled. Did she miss the security of a home and a steady income, she wondered? Yes . . . if she had to be honest, she did. But she was learning to find her security in trusting that Jesus would fulfil all his promises. He had told them not to be anxious, not to worry about tomorrow, but to seek his kingdom and his righteousness first and foremost . . . he knew what they needed. She looked up at her husband. Was that a tear rolling down his cheek?

"Oh Peter," she said wiping away the tear, "I love you so much."

"And I you," he said drawing her closer still.

They stood there, silently watching the ship sail away until it was barely visible.

"I suppose we had better start our journey to Lydda," Peter said, suddenly becoming aware of the people staring at them.

"They are not accustomed to seeing a husband showing affection to his wife in public," Perpetua laughed.

"Oh," Peter said, dropping his arm, but not letting go of her hand, "well . . . Jesus said we would be known as his followers by our love, no?"

They both giggled as they walked away from the harbour.

∗ ∗ ∗

"And then Peter said, 'Aeneas, stand up and put your mat in its place. Jesus has healed you.' And he did. Many in Lydda and Sharon who saw him, came to believe in Jesus," Perpetua was telling Simon's wife, Elizabeth,[9] about their journey.

"So, it is not only the resurrection of Dorcas,[10] the Lord is doing great wonders through your husband," Elizabeth replied. "And it means so much to Simon to have you stay with us . . . most people avoid a tanner's home, that's why we live well outside the city walls.[11] And do you know, some rabbis have even said that they will allow the wives of tanners to divorce them because of the odour!"

"I understand, believe me. Some people in Capernaum would not visit us either . . . they said our home reeked of fish even though we sold most of our fish at the harbour or in the marketplace . . . but not Jesus. He never seemed to have a problem with all those clean and unclean rules. Strange, don't you think? He who was altogether holy . . . touching the lepers, associating with the prostitutes and so-called sinners."

"What I find strange is that anyone could read the Scriptures and still think of themselves as better than others. What do they make of 'there is no one that does good, not a single one'?"[12]

"Or, 'who could stand if the Lord kept a record of sins'?"[13]

---

9. We don't know if Simon the tanner was married or not. This is simply for the sake of the narrative.

10. For parallels between Peter and the prophets Elijah and Elisha, see 1 Kings 17:19, 23 and 2 Kings 4:10, 32–35.

11. Because tanners worked with the dead bodies of animals, they were considered ceremonially unclean. Both Jews and Gentiles also found the odor associated with the tanning process to be offensive. For these reasons, most tanners had to live outside of the city.

12. Psalm 14:3; 53:3; Romans 3:12.

13. Psalm 130:3.

"We have all sinned . . . we are all unclean before him. Even our best attempts are like dirty rags in his sight.[14] We are all equally in need of forgiveness . . . so how can anyone look down on another? The ground is level before a holy God."

"Peter always refers to himself as a fellow elder . . . he does not like it when people treat him as if he is more important than others."

"Yes, I have noticed that . . . and I think that is what we all like about him. He is humble."

"He has never forgotten where he came from, a lowly fisherman . . . but he has also never forgotten that regardless of how willing the spirit might be, the flesh remains weak.[15] He loves to quote the proverb, 'God opposes the proud, but is gracious to the humble.'[16] And this is what he seeks to instil in those he teaches . . . he wants them to copy him in humility and obedience and trust."

"I do hope that all our future leaders will lead by example," Elizabeth said. "It is always easier to follow those who do what they say . . . I imagine that was what Jesus was like?"

"Actually, one could say what Jesus is like. That's what he promised us. That he would be with us even to the end of time.[17] In a sense he still walks before us . . . leading us, guiding us, through his Spirit in us. So, we still follow where he has already been, if that makes any sense at all."

"Yes, it does. I've noticed that you and Peter spend hours in prayer every evening and every morning . . . I . . . I must confess I have listened to your prayers. I have heard you asking him to show you where he is working in the hearts and minds of people."

"Our prayers are not private . . . actually I am glad you overheard our prayers, as that will help you to pray in a similar manner. God is always at work. Jesus once said that the Father is always working and that he simply joined in doing what was already being done, that he could only do what he saw the Father doing . . . that without the Father he could do nothing.[18] We must believe that as the Father showed Jesus what to do so he will still do the same with us today. The enemy wants to make us blind to this reality."

"So, you are saying that if we ask the Father to show us where he is already at work in the lives of those around us, he will?"

"That's exactly what I'm saying, yes."

---

14. Isaiah 64:6.

15. Matthew 26:41.

16. Proverbs 3:34.

17. Matthew 28:20.

18. John 5:17, 19.

"That is so assuring . . . bringing others to faith in him is not up to us . . . we are merely the vehicles through which God works, right?"

"Yes. We believe that the Holy Spirit alone can break up the fallow ground of our stony hearts.[19] Only he can convict the world of its sin, only he can show them God's righteousness, only he can make them aware of judgement.[20] But it is our responsibility to preach the word . . . we must always be prepared to give an answer to those who ask us to give them a reason for our hope in Jesus.[21] That is our role . . . he does the rest . . . only God can turn the hearts of people."

"This has been such a precious time. Thank you. We are so blessed to have you stay with us."

"And we are blessed to be here."

"Our husbands must be hungry, shall we take them some—" Elizabeth was interrupted by a loud banging on the gate outside. "Now, who is that at the gate?"

"Shall I go and see? Oh, never mind . . . Peter is already there," Perpetua said, looking through the window.

"Who is it?"

"No one we know. There are three men . . . Peter is ushering them in."

"Oh. Well then, we had better prepare more food."

* * *

"Reptiles too?" Elizabeth asked, making a face. Peter was telling the group about the vision he had seen while on the roof of Simon and Elizabeth's home in Joppa.

"Everything we Jews would consider as unclean," Peter replied, "and as this sheet full of these beasts was lowered down before me, I heard a voice instructing me to rise up, slaughter these animals, and eat them."

"You all need to know that my husband has never eaten anything unclean – he has always followed the dietary laws, even as a boy," Perpetua emphasized.

"That's exactly what I said . . . but then the voice told me not to call unclean what God has declared clean."

"What does that mean?" Simon asked.

"Well . . ." Peter looked a bit embarrassed as he glanced over at the three guests. One was a Roman soldier and the other two were gentile servants.

The Roman soldier smiled, "We know you Jews consider us unclean."

---

19. Hosea 10:12.

20. John 16:8.

21. 1 Peter 3:15.

"Yes, well," Peter cleared his throat. "I believe that is exactly what our Lord was trying to tell me. I ought not to call unclean what he has made clean."

"I think Peter has already taken a giant step forward by inviting you three to stay the night," Elizabeth said in Peter's defence.

"For which we are very grateful," the soldier said, "to all of you." The servants nodded in agreement but said nothing. It was not their place to be vocal in company.

"But tell us, why have you come looking for me?" Peter asked.

"Cornelius, the centurion," the soldier began, "the head of the Italian regiment in Caesarea . . . he and his family are devout, god-fearing people."

"He is a righteous man and is respected by all the Jews in Caesarea," the servant suddenly blurted out, forgetting himself. His companion nudged him viciously in the ribs.

The soldier eyed the servant and smiled, "Indeed, he is . . . even his servants are devoted to him. Well, he had a vision in which an angel of God appeared to him and told him to send men to Joppa to find you, Peter. The angel even told him where you were staying . . . he was very specific. We are meant to bring you back with us to Caesarea."

"And we will come," Peter replied. "The Lord told me not to hesitate to go with you."

"Oh, lovely," Perpetua said, "perhaps we can find Philip and his family while we are there, Peter?"

"Yes, that's a good idea. Well, if you will excuse us, we would like to get some rest before the journey tomorrow."

"Oh, Peter, it is not that far," Perpetua teased.

"I know, but I . . . we also need to pray. I need to know what our Lord is doing if I am to be of any use to him."

"Indeed. You are right." Turning to their hosts and their guests, Perpetua said, "We do hope you all get a good night's rest."

"I've never been to Joppa before," the silent servant said suddenly. "Forgive me, but may we . . . ?"

"Certainly," Simon said, "I will take you myself. Come. I will show you our small harbour as well. You might want to wrap your travel cloak around you. The sea breeze can be chilly."

* * *

A messenger met them on the way to tell Peter that Cornelius was expecting them and that he had gathered all his friends and family together in his large home. A few believers from Joppa had decided to go along with them. As Peter entered the compound, Cornelius prostrated himself before him.

"Oh, no, please," Peter stooped down to help Cornelius to his feet, "please, I am only a man . . . please do not pay me reverence."

"Forgive me . . . after the angelic visitation, I am rather nervous. We know so little . . . but please. Where are my manners? Come inside."

As they entered the home, Peter saw that a rather large crowd had gathered together. "I am entering a Gentile home," he thought to himself, "but in the vision . . ."

"You are the first Jew to enter my home," Cornelius interrupted his thoughts, "we are honoured. Thank you for coming."

Peter smiled. It must be as awkward for Cornelius as it was for him.

"Yes," Peter said, addressing the whole group, "it is true. You know our laws well. It is forbidden for a Jew to enter the house of a Gentile. But the day before yesterday[22] God showed me in a vision that I am not to think of anyone as unclean or impure. That is why I came without hesitation." Then turning back to Cornelius he asked, "but please tell me. Why have you sent for me?"

"A few days ago . . . let's see . . . yes, it was four days ago, I was praying . . . I am what you Jews call a God-fearer.[23] But suddenly there was this large, shining being standing before me. He told me that God has heard my prayers and that he was well pleased with my gifts to the destitute . . . but then he said I should send for you. He gave me very clear instructions as to where you could be found . . . and so, as you know, I dispatched a soldier and two servants to ask you to come to us. Well, now you are here – again thank you for coming – and we are gathered in the presence of our God to hear whatever it is you have to tell us."

Peter cleared his throat. He had never spoken to a group of Gentiles before . . . but as this group was made up of God-fearers, they no doubt knew some of the Scriptures. He began by relating common knowledge about Jesus of Nazareth. The miracles of Jesus were still a topic of conversation among many. Then he told them about the crucifixion . . . about Jesus's death and burial, and about the resurrection. He reminded them that many had seen Jesus alive and that he was one of the witnesses chosen by the Lord to tell others that God

---

22. "Peter's trip from Joppa to Caesarea, a distance of 40 miles, took two days (Acts 10:23–24)." Edwin M. Yamauchi, "On the Road with Paul," *Christian History Magazine* 47, online, https://christianhistoryinstitute.org/magazine/article/on-the-road-with-paul.

23. God-fearers were Gentiles who believed in the God of Israel and observed most Jewish rites and traditions, but stopped short of becoming full converts, usually because of their reluctance to submit to the requirement of circumcision.

had appointed Jesus to be the Judge of both the living and the dead. "And," he added, "all who believe in Jesus receive forgiveness of sins through his name."

Peter had barely finished his sentence when the Holy Spirit fell on the Gentiles before him. He turned to the believers who had come with him from Joppa and saw that they were as astonished as he was. There was no denying that God had poured out his Spirit on the Gentiles, just as he had on the Jews. So this, then, was what the Lord meant when he said that he ought not to call unclean what God has declared clean!

"I do not believe anyone can prevent these people from being baptized in the name of Jesus since God has already baptized them with his Holy Spirit! Who can deny them the sign when they already have the seal?" Peter said to the other believers.

There was such joy as each new believer symbolically died with Jesus and was raised to new life in him. Peter stayed there for a number of days, instructing them more clearly in the way and introducing them to Philip and the other believers in Caesarea.

* * *

"But Peter, you willingly and knowingly entered a Gentile home and had a meal with them!"

Peter and Perpetua had just returned to Jerusalem and were taken aback by the criticism they received for what had occurred in Caesarea. Peter explained to them exactly what had happened, starting with his vision while he was on the rooftop in Joppa, and then walking them through each successive event up until the unexpected outpouring of the Holy Spirit upon the Gentiles.

After he had told them that the Lord had poured out the Holy Spirit on the group without requiring circumcision or any other religious rite, they had no further concerns.

"So then," James said, "it appears that God has granted eternal life even to the Gentiles."

"Yes," Peter said curtly, "so it appears."

The two men walked out into the bright Jerusalem sunlight.

"Peter, we can't be too careful," James said softly, turning to face Peter.

"I know, I know . . . we have already had to deal with the likes of Simon Magus in Samaria."

"Exactly . . . although we hear he is no longer in Samaria. Apparently, he has gone to Rome."

"That is what we heard as well. It is disconcerting, don't you think?" Peter paused. Would now be the right moment to reveal their plans? He remembered the Scripture that said there was wisdom in the multitude of counsellors,[24] so he decided to press on and tell his friend.

"We have been praying and thinking about . . ." Peter hesitated, still unsure.

"Yes?"

"James, would you pray with me, please?"

"I would be happy to pray with you, Peter . . . but what are we praying for?"

"I believe Perpetua and I need to go to Rome."[25]

James was silent for a moment. Then he said, "If you do go, I would dare to ask you to take my brother with you."

"Jude?"[26]

"Together with Rachel, his wife.[27] Yes. It will do them the world of good to get out of the city for a time . . . besides, he has much to learn from you."

* * *

24. Proverbs 11:14; 15:22; 24:6.

25. Various early church traditions have Peter in Rome as early as the second year of Claudius.

26. As there are a number of similarities between 2 Peter and the epistle of Jude, I believe there may have been a prolonged time of interaction between Peter and the Lord's brother, both of whom, we are told in 1 Corinthians 9:5 travelled with their wives and were known to the Corinthian believers.

27. Paul indicates that not only Peter, but also the Lord's brothers took along their wives on their missionary journeys. I have used the name Rachel for the sake of the narrative.

13

To Rome and Back

Open the gate, Rhoda!" Mark was banging on the entrance to his mother's compound. There was a sense of urgency in his voice. "Rhoda!" he shouted. The gate opened. "Finally! What took you so long?"

"I have other duties, too, you know."

"Is it true?"

"Is what true?"

"Are they back?"

"Who?"

"Rhoda!"

"I'm just teasing you. Yes. They are back. They are with your mother and Silas."

Mark bounded up the stairs to the upper room. "Peter!" They fell into each other arms and hugged each other warmly.

"I can't wait to hear your stories! Where did you go? Did you go all the way to Rome? What was it like? Weren't you afraid? Did the people believe you when you told them about Jesus? Oh, how I wish I had gone with you!"

"Slow down! Slow down, Mark!" Peter laughed, "How I have missed your youthful exuberance!"

"He reminds me of a younger you."

"Oh, hello, Perpetua. Forgive me . . . I didn't see you. It is dark in here after the bright sunlight outside! Where's Petronila?"

"She decided to stay in Rome. She has many friends there," Perpetua said, motioning with her hand that Mark should come and greet her properly.

Mark knelt down next to where Perpetua was reclining and kissed her hastily on both cheeks. Then he jumped up and turned back to face Peter.

"Don't keep me in such suspense. Tell me, please!"

"My son," Mary laughed as she spoke, "Peter and Perpetua only got back an hour ago. They haven't even finished their refreshments. Give them a little time to catch their breath."

"Oh, hello mother . . . oh, and Silas! My, this is quite the gathering!" Mark exclaimed, hastily greeting first his mother and then his friend.

"Peter—"

"Mark," his mother interrupted, holding up a hand in admonition.

"No, no . . . let him ask all he likes," Peter chuckled. "Jesus always loved it when we showed an interest . . . by asking many questions!" They all laughed. "Silas and I were just talking about writing a letter to the believers in the churches Perpetua and I visited while on this trip. Perhaps you can help us?"

"Help? Me? I'd be honoured! Thank you. Yes! Which churches? Where did you go from here? Start from the very beginning. I don't want to miss a single word."

"Well . . . let me see. You remember when I had to defend myself with regard to the conversion of Cornelius, his family, and his friends?"

"Yes. I remember. They all wanted them to become Jews first . . . to follow all the rules and regulations required of those who wish to accept the faith. But you said . . ."

"That if God accepted the Gentiles by pouring out the promised Holy Spirit upon them, who were we to lay extra burdens on them. Yes. My, it feels like an age has gone by since that day." Peter paused for a moment. "So, when we left Jerusalem – that is Perpetua, Petronilla, Jude, Rachel, and I – we travelled north to Caesarea—"

"Did you see Philip?"[1] Mark interjected.

"Yes, we did. He has a house there now."

"He has four daughters," Perpetua said looking at Mark playfully.

"Four *unmarried* daughters," Peter emphasized with a smile, "and did I mention that they are all quite attractive?"

"They all are very gifted too . . . they have an active prophetic ministry," Perpetua added with a twinkle in her eyes.

Mark turned crimson. Silas reached over and ruffled Mark's hair.

"Stop, please . . ." Mark said pulling away.

"But," Peter continued, "the primary reason for going to Caesarea was to see how Cornelius and the growing church in his home was getting along."

"How are they? Still growing in the faith?"

---

1. Acts 21:8–9.

"Yes. Very much so. They have witnessed to many and there were quite a few people we had not yet met."

"That's wonderful," Mary said, relaxing a bit and reclining at the table herself. "You bring one man to faith and he brings many. You are multiplying yourself."

"And it was Cornelius who first put the idea of going to Rome in his head," Perpetua said, smiling.

"Really? Why?" Mark asked enthralled.

"Well, he was of the Italian regiment, remember, and he still had many connections in Rome," Peter explained, "and he wanted to see them freed from superstition and fear. Remember, we had all heard rumours about Simon Magus spreading his poison in Rome by that time. So, he resigned his post and went with us on to Antioch."[2]

"You helped establish the house church there, Peter. Tell me about that, please."

"But that was long ago . . . I told you about that . . . didn't I?"

"I wasn't with you at the time, remember? That was when Saul came back to Jerusalem after his return to Damascus . . . and I never got a chance to ask you about it. So many other things happened in between."

"Ah, yes. I remember. Well . . . as you no doubt know already, the community there was really founded by believers who fled from the persecution in Jerusalem after our brother Stephen was martyred. We simply helped them get a bit more organized.[3] Most of them were Jews at that time, or at least proselytes to Judaism, but we know that after we left, some believers from Cyprus and Cyrene witnessed to the Greeks also, and that they became believers and joined the church."[4]

"Yes, we heard about that," Mary said. "They decided to send Barnabas to Antioch,[5] just like they sent you, Peter, to Samaria when the Samaritans believed the preaching of Philip.[6] He has written to say that it is quite a diverse community."

---

2. This is fictional yet based on tradition.

3. This is according to Orthodox tradition: "Church tradition maintains that the See of Antioch was founded by Saint Peter the Apostle in A.D. 34." Antiochian Orthodox Christian Archdiocese of North America, "The Patriarchate of Antioch: Founded by Saints Peter and Paul," http://ww1.antiochian.org/patofant. See also, "Is There Any Evidence to Support the Claim that the Apostle St. Peter Founded the Church in Antioch and, if so, What Are the Implications?" StackExchange, Christianity, https://christianity.stackexchange.com/questions/68875/is-there-any-evidence-to-support-the-claim-that-the-apostle-st-peter-founded-th.

4. Acts 11:19–21.

5. Acts 11:22.

6. Acts 8:14.

"Yes," Peter said, "it is . . . quite diverse. We stopped there briefly on our way back here. Saul is with him now. Apparently, Barnabas went to Tarsus to find him and brought him back to Antioch. They are both doing very well, actually. But I'm going to get you confused with our going and coming. Back to the story. From Antioch we continued north to Cappadocia."[7]

"Why Cappadocia?" Mark enquired.

"For the same reasons we went to Antioch," Peter replied. "There were some Jewish believers there who were converted in Jerusalem at the Feast of Pentecost . . . some of them had been God-fearers and proselytes before, although most were born Jews. But since they returned home, they had been joined by others fleeing the persecution . . . the same persecution that served as the spark for the planting of the church in Antioch . . . the one that happened here after Stephen was stoned to death."

"What is it like, this place . . . Cappadocia?" Mark enquired.

"A strange land . . . a beautiful land, but a strange land. There are these elongated rock formations . . . I've never seen anything like it. They look like giant cones or like big chimneys. People have carved out homes for themselves in some of the larger rocks, there are even stables for their livestock in some of them."

"People live inside rocks?" Mark asked, not meaning to sound sceptical, "I've seen tombs carved out of rocks, but homes?"

"Yes. Surprising, no?" Peter replied, smiling. "But think about it. What a wonderful picture of us being inside Jesus. Jesus is the Rock and we find refuge in him."

"Yes," Mary said, "that is a wonderful picture. It makes one feel safe and secure."

"And then? Where did you go from there?" Mark pressed on.

"Well, then we travelled on through Galatia and Pontus and Bithynia for the same reasons," Perpetua added. "There are many young believers scattered throughout that region and they all needed to be encouraged."

"Yes, think about it," Peter said, "the first group left so soon after they became believers at the Feast of Pentecost. They didn't have time to be properly instructed in the Way.[8] But then, it wasn't long after they had started meeting in their homes, that they were joined by this new group who were fleeing persecution . . . and they brought with them more of our verbal instruction . . .

---

7. Eusebius of Caesarea, *Ecclesiastical History* 2.9.1–4; 2.14.6, 15–16.

8. Before believers were called Christians, they were known as followers of the Way. See Acts 9:2; 24:14.

you remember, Mark . . . you were part of that small group. And to think I never knew that all the while you were writing down whatever I said on any scrap of parchment you could find."

"Yes, I remember that small group well. Just so you know, thanks to those discussions we had with Matthew and the others, I have rewritten my notes now to make them neater and more readable . . . that all seems like years ago now. But, please tell us, how are my former fellow students doing? Have they remained faithful?"

"They have . . . and more," Perpetua said. "They have been preaching to the Gentiles as well. The community has been growing . . . both in numbers and in depth. The Jews among them still have access to the Scriptures in the synagogues, so they teach the others. And – what Peter failed to mention earlier – they have been most recently joined by some Jews from Rome . . . there have been rumours that Emperor Claudius will expel all Jews from the city because of the constant arguments about Jesus[9] . . . but it remains to be seen if he will do that. However, some of these new settlers are believers . . . but not all of them. And there are some who are quite confused as to the truth about Jesus and, in their confusion, they are misleading others."

"This is why I feel we need to write a letter to our brethren there. They still had so many questions when we left them," Peter added.

The group sat in silence for a while. But curiosity got the better of Mark.

"And then?" he blurted out, his eyes darting around the table to see if anyone objected to his enthusiasm, "Where did you go then?"

"Well, we travelled through a number of other cities on the way. Cornelius and his family stayed behind in the city of Skepsis, close to Ephesus.[10] You would be amazed how fiery a preacher he has become! We found a few believers in Corinth too . . . all from Jewish backgrounds, but I believe that Gentile believers have been added to their number by now."[11]

"And Rome? Did you go to Rome from there?" Mark was so excited; he could barely sit still.

---

9. Acts 18:2; Suetonius also wrote: "He banished from Rome all the Jews, who were continually making disturbances at the instigation of one Chrestus." Alexander Thomson, "C. Suetonius Tranquillus, *Divus Claudius*," *Divus Claudius* 25, http://www.perseus.tufts.edu/hopper/text?doc=Perseus:abo:phi,1348,015:25.

10. "Tradition . . . teaches that Cornelius retired from the army and accompanied Peter as they preached the Gospel." Angelo Stagnaro, "What Do We Know About St. Cornelius the Centurion?" *National Catholic Register* blog, 2 February 2017, https://www.ncregister.com/blog/astagnaro/what-do-we-know-about-st.-cornelius-the-centurion.

11. Paul mentions a "Cephas" faction in Corinth in 1 Corinthians 1:13.

"Yes," Peter laughed, "we sailed on to Rome."[12] His expression suddenly changed, and he became more serious, "It is an impressive city, Mark . . . beautiful buildings, wide streets, a large marketplace . . . but it is a very sad city too. There is so much poverty . . . and such superstition! People live in fear of the many gods, and of the emperor. I had thought that Cornelius would have gone with us all the way to the imperial city – and, indeed, I wanted him to go with us as I do not speak Latin well at all – but he believed he was called of God to remain in Skepsis. Thankfully he gave us a few names, didn't he, my dear wife?" Peter said.

"Yes, he did!" Perpetua said, her face lighting up as she remembered. "Especially that beautiful family and their son, Clement.[13] He is not altogether unlike you, Mark . . . so many questions . . . like a dry sponge sucking up as much water as possible. Petronilla, Rachel, and Jude are staying with the family while we are away. He became our chief interpreter."

"Yes, a remarkable young man he is," Peter added. "He will be a leader in the church one day, that is for sure. But Mark . . . you are fluent in Latin too, are you not?"[14]

"Yes, I am," Mark replied, blushing. "Father thought I ought to be fluent in many languages and so I studied Latin from an early age."

"Perhaps you ought to come with us next time . . . as you already know my sermons and lectures well."

"Oh, yes! I'd love to go with you. Mother, may I? Please?"

"We can talk about this later," Mary replied, startled by the sudden request.

"Yes, mother." Mark glanced down for a moment, clearly disappointed by his mother's reaction, and then turned back to face Peter, "But tell me, do people really believe that Romulus and Remus were brought up by a she-wolf? That is such a strange story."

"Yes . . . some believe that," Peter replied, "but you must remember, Mark, that when people do not know the truth, they will believe anything."

"Like the lies of Simon Magus, you mean?" Silas enquired.

---

12. See, "Ancient Syriac Documents: The Teaching of Simon Cephas in the City of Rome," in Roberts and Donaldson, *The Ante-Nicene Fathers*, 637.

13. Clement of Rome. Philippians 4:3. See Diane Severance, "Clement of Rome," Christianity.com, 28 April 2010, https://www.christianity.com/church/church-history/timeline/1-300/clement-of-rome-11629592.html.

14. Mark was well versed in Latin. See Lane, *Gospel According to Mark*, 24.

"Like the lies of Simon Magus, yes," Peter said. "He has since departed this world . . . but unfortunately, his false teaching lives on in his followers."[15]

"It sounds like Rome is a place I would not want to visit," Mark said, trying to convince himself after his mother's refusal.

"No, no . . . make no mistake, Rome is a key city for the spread of the good news about Jesus. And, besides, it is an attractive city, built on seven hills, on the left bank of the river Tiber. There used to be a lot of old swamps in between the rivers, but they have drained them all now . . . even so, that area is still prone to flooding in heavy rains."

"The weather is warm, but not oppressively so, because it is close to the sea," Perpetua added.

"As you can see, my dear wife fell in love with the city," Peter joked.

"No," Perpetua chuckled, "no, not with the city. I fell in love with the people. I think the Lord Jesus gave me a little of his infinite compassion before he ascended to heaven."

"She has managed to fill our home with many little orphans," Peter said smiling.

"And many abandoned babies," she added. "It is frightful how many women give birth to their babies and then abandon them in the wild . . . sometimes even in the streets. Some say they are making an offering to the gods. Imagine. How can a mother abandon a child she carried in her womb for so many months?"

"Some of them are destitute," Peter said. "We ought to do better in providing a home for those who have none."

"Yes, that's true," Perpetua said wistfully. "We are trying. That is what is weighing heavily on Petronilla's heart. She wants to reach out to the many women who themselves have been abandoned and show them the love and acceptance of our Lord."

"Enough questions for now," Mary said. "You both need to rest. I remember well how you enjoyed a nap at noon, Peter!"

"I was praying, Mary!" Peter laughed.[16] "Just like I need to pray now before we write this letter!"

---

15. There are several legends regarding Simon Magus in Rome. One has him ascending into heaven before Emperor Nero only to fall to the ground through the intercession of the apostle Peter and Paul. Another has him agreeing to be buried so that he might rise again on the third day where he remained. But there is no historic basis for these claims.

16. Acts 10:9–10.

"So you say," she teased, "but come. Rest a while. Mark . . . I need you to help me prepare the food for this evening.[17] Go to the market and see if anything arrived recently from the Galilee region."

"Yes, mother," he said reluctantly, "but after the nap we will write the letter, yes?"

"Yes, Mark . . . after *prayer*," Peter emphasized. He yawned and gave an exaggerated stretch. "But your mother is right. We need a little rest too."

"Not me," Perpetua said, "I will help prepare the food."

* * *

---

17. It was customary to have two meals per day, a mid-morning breakfast and dinner before sunset. Meals consisted mostly of dried, salted fish, different kinds of fruit, nuts, various cheeses, honey, olives and olive oil, legumes, and various types of grain. Meat was eaten rarely. See "Jewish Food: Eating in Historical Jerusalem," Jewish Virtual Library, https://www.jewishvirtuallibrary. org/eating-in-historical-jerusalem.

14

Pastoral Writing

Did you have a good rest?" Mary asked when Peter returned.
"Yes, I did, thank you . . . *and* I prayed."

"Any visions? White sheets from heaven?"

"Yes, I had a vision of a mocking woman . . ."

"And just who might that woman be?" Mark laughed.

"Not a word from you, young man!" his mother scolded.

"Where is Perpetua?" Peter asked.

"Oh, she just nipped out quickly to see Dorcas."[1]

"Dorcas? Is she living in Jerusalem now?"

"No, she is visiting family here."

"Well, I need my wife. I cannot write that letter without her input. She gives me such wonderful advice. That is why I take her with me on all my trips."[2]

"Is that why you take me?" Perpetua said, walking in at that moment, "And all this time, I thought it was because you loved me."

"That too," Peter said, smiling. "Now, come. Where is Silas? He needs to write this down. His Greek is so much better than mine."

"I'm here," Silas said, entering the room, "I just need someone to check my spelling though. Mark?"

"Me?"

"Yes, you know Greek better than anyone here."

"Well, I'm not so sure about that, but I'll sit next to you and look over your shoulder."

"So, where do we begin?" Silas asked, sitting like a ready scribe, legs crossed, wooden board resting on his legs with the scroll ready and his pen poised.

---

1. Acts 9:36–41.
2. 1 Corinthians 9:5.

"Peter, one sent by Jesus Christ," Peter began thoughtfully, "to those chosen by God, pilgrims and pioneers of the faith through dispersion."

"That's a great start, my dearest husband. Nothing wrong with your Greek."

Peter smiled but said nothing. Perpetua was a born encourager.

"But now living in Pontus, Galatia, Cappadocia, Asia, and Bithynia?" Silas suggested.

"Yes," Peter replied. He paused and then added, "chosen out of the world by God the Father by means of the hallowing work of the Holy Spirit, for a life of obedience to Jesus Christ, effected by the sprinkling of his blood."

"That is a reference to the sprinkling of the blood of the sacrifice on the people of Israel in the wilderness, is it?"[3] Silas asked, while scribbling furiously.

"Very good, Silas. Yes, Moses sprinkled the blood on the people after they promised to be obedient to everything God commanded. Followers of Jesus must pledge allegiance to him . . . they must learn to obey all that he has taught us.[4] Now, add, 'May grace and peace be multiplied toward you.'"

"In abundance," Perpetua added.

"Yes, in abundance," said Peter beaming at his wife. Peter closed his eyes as if needing to concentrate. Then he began to dictate. He spoke out a blessing to God who had chosen them by his merciful and gracious intervention through the death and resurrection of Jesus. Even though many of them had to leave behind homes and possessions as they fled from those who sought to stamp out the faith, they had received an eternal inheritance kept for them in heaven. With tender words, he comforted those who were grieving because of all they had suffered. He reminded them that the sages and prophets had longed to understand the nature of the salvation they had received when they believed the preaching of the apostles on the day the Holy Spirit was sent from heaven[5] . . . things even the angels longed to comprehend. In this gentle fashion, Peter continued to instruct them with regard to the manner in which they ought to conduct themselves as followers of a holy God. His reasoning was clear . . . they had been reborn into a completely new life . . . an incorruptible and eternal life. He told them to love each other, as they were now born of one who loved them enough to give them what they could not earn for themselves. His speech was filled with quotations and allusions to the writings of the sages.

---

3. Exodus 24:7–8.

4. Matthew 28:20.

5. This may be a reference to the day of Pentecost and thus the day of their conversion to Christ.

"Oh, how I have missed your teaching, Peter," Mary said, wiping away a tear. "You are so kind and gentle . . . just like the shepherd Jesus told us about . . . gently nurturing his lambs."

"This group has been through a lot," Perpetua said. "Now they are facing all sorts of problems with their neighbours, both Jews and Gentiles alike."

"Yes," Peter said, "I must address that. First, they must learn not to retaliate. They need to lay aside all their anger and any residual bitterness, they must resist any form of play acting . . . they must not be envious and certainly not slander anyone."

"They need to drink deeply from the sweet milk of the word," Mark said. "Just like you taught us, Peter. That's the only way to grow . . . that's the only way to become like him."

"That's good," said Silas, "should I include what Mark just said?"

"Yes," Peter said, "and then write . . . let me think . . . yes. 'You have been drawn to the cornerstone that was rejected by men but chosen as precious by God.'[6] Yes. That will let them see that God is not indifferent . . . he understands what it feels like to be cast aside by your own people." Peter continued to build them up with encouraging words, telling them that they were now like living stones that God was using to build a new temple . . . not one made with earthly materials, but with individual believers knit together in one holy community. As he had told the Samaritans so many years ago, he now told the believers in Asia that they were the new Israel of God . . . a royal priesthood . . . a holy nation through whom God would make himself known to all peoples. They were to be different because they had been taken out from the kingdom of darkness and transferred into the gracious light of God . . . they were now his own people and therefore they ought to be like him in every way, so that through their behaviour, others may bring glory to God.[7]

"They need to be obedient citizens too, Peter," Perpetua said. "They must silence all the accusations against them through doing what is good and right."

"Yes, that's right. Are you getting this Silas?"

"Yes, but we can go through it again later before I make the final copy."

"We will need to make a few copies so that each house church can receive a personal letter from us," Perpetua urged.

"Indeed, we must," Peter said and then continued, "they must remember that while it is true that they have been set free from slavery to sin, they are

---

6. Isaiah 28:16.
7. See Deuteronomy 10:15; Isaiah 62:12; Hosea 1:9–10.

now slaves to God. So, they must be respectful toward all; they must love the community; they must revere God; and they must honour the emperor."

"And those who are still enslaved to others?" Perpetua enquired.

"Yes . . . a sad reality, but hopefully one that we followers of Jesus will bring to an end in the near future," Peter replied. "But for the time being . . . those who are slaves ought to be obedient to their masters regardless of their master's character." Peter spoke about the patient endurance of Jesus who suffered even though he had done no wrong. Jesus never retaliated.[8]

In his mind's eye Peter was taken back to that dreaded night in the high priest's courtyard. At that time he could not understand why the one who could command the wind to cease and the demons to leave and the dead to rise, why he did nothing to defend himself as they hurled their abuse at him . . . beating him and mocking him. But he knew now that he bore every blow for him . . . for his children . . . for the world. It was through his suffering – his death on that cross – that humanity could be set free. In so many ways, Jesus was now that tree of life spoken of in the first book of Moses . . . eat of me, drink of me, Jesus had said on that night when he was betrayed. He was the shepherd giving up his life for his sheep.

"Peter?"

"What?"

"Are you still with us?"

"Oh, yes, yes . . . I was remembering . . ." He went on to tell them his thoughts, they had heard the story before, one of great failure, but failure that led to great humility.

After a brief pause, Perpetua said, "I'd like us to say something that might encourage those wives we met. Remember, Peter? Those believing women married to unbelieving men. Through their pure living, they need to show their husbands the truth . . . to work on inner beauty, not external beauty. We need to urge them to imitate the holy women of the past . . . like Sarah."

"Yes, and we need to remind the believing husbands that the curse that brought about division between men and women has been abolished through Jesus,"[9] Peter added. "They are to exercise their God-given authority as co-heirs of Jesus . . . as complimentary and yet as equals. If they oppress their wives,

---

8. Isaiah 53:7–9; cf. John 15:20; Matthew 10:24–25.

9. Compare Genesis 1:26–28 and Genesis 2:20b–24 (gender complimentary equality) with Genesis 3:16b (gender division and inequality). Then read Joel 2:28–29 and Galatians 3:28. In the last days, or in the new covenant period, gender equality would be restored as the curse has been removed in Christ.

their prayers will be hindered. In fact, Jesus cannot and will not bless any form of abuse against women . . . any women, not just wives."

Peter continued to admonish the recipients of his letter to live in peace and harmony with each other. Quoting from the Psalms, he told them that this was the way to receive blessing from God. He told them to always be ready to defend the faith . . . to give a persuasive reason for the hope they possessed through that faith. Again he spoke about the purpose of suffering, that through suffering salvation had been achieved, not just for them, but also for all those who had been kept in the collective place of the dead . . . those who had believed that one day they would be set free from death. He likened the new creation, brought about by Jesus, to the earth after the flood – just as the flood purged the earth of all wickedness, so too, baptism symbolically cleansed them and gave them new life through participation in the resurrection of Jesus. "And Jesus is now seated as reigning king at the right hand of God . . . angels, archangels, principalities, and powers . . . all are subject to him and his rule."

"What you are basically saying, Peter," Mark chimed in, "is that they ought to imitate Jesus . . . that they ought to have the same mind as him."

"Yes, the time for obedience to a worldly way of life is over. We must all live for Jesus. We can no longer imitate the pagans . . . we cannot live as they live and do what they do. Yes, believers will suffer for it, because the pagans will not understand . . . they will be mocked and abused. But they must always remember that they will have to explain their behaviour to the Judge of all humanity . . . past, present, and future."

"So we must all live to God through the power of the Holy Spirit," Perpetua added.

"That's right, the old ways are coming to an end. In the meantime, we need to care for each other – we need to use the gifts God has given to each one of us so that we might build up our community. There are trials to come . . . that they must understand," Peter added, his voice taking on an urgent tone. "There will be a time when their faith will be tested as by fire. But they must not suffer as evildoers . . . it is only when they suffer as followers of Christ that he is glorified. Judgement always begins with us, God's own people, and we can only be saved from such a judgement by God's gracious will . . . by committing our souls to him in doing what is right regardless of the consequences."

"You need to address the leaders among them, as well, my husband."

"Yes, but I do not want to sound like someone who lords it over them. I am a fellow leader with them . . . true, I am an eyewitness to the sufferings of Jesus but still . . . I am merely a simple shepherd of shepherds who can only urge them to tend the flock entrusted to their care, even as he cares for us all."

He addressed the leaders and the flock in general, telling them to seek after humility as it was only through being humbled that God would lift them up in his time. He told them to lay all anxious thoughts and every cause for concern at his feet, urging them to be watchful, for the evil one prowled about in search of those he could destroy. "They ought to resist him at all times," he said, "as Satan would try to sow doubt among them . . . make them think that they were the only one's suffering . . . that somehow God had abandoned them."

Then Peter ended with a beautiful doxology, a hymn of praise to the God who alone could establish them and make them what they could be in him.

For a while, they all sat in silence, contemplating the greatness of God and his infinite graciousness in Jesus.

"How should I end the letter?" Silas eventually asked.

"Ah, yes . . . tell them the letter comes from me via your hand. Also tell them that their fellow believers in Babylon send greetings."[10]

"Babylon?" Silas asked.

"Yes, Babylon . . . they will understand," Peter replied. Peter told them about the time when Jesus had spoken out against Jerusalem. How little he had understood back then . . . but Jesus had clearly said that Jerusalem had become apostate and ripe for judgement . . . the name Babylon was a fitting

---

10. 1 Peter has a positive view of the Roman government (1 Peter 2:13–14). In this light, equating Rome with Babylon, an evil, oppressive, or repressive power, does not make sense. I believe the letter is addressed to newish believers, Hellenistic (1 Peter 4:3–5) Jewish followers of Jesus in the provinces of Asia Minor, more than likely converted at Pentecost as those nations were all present in Jerusalem that day, not believers in Rome. It seems likely that others joined them later during the persecution following the murder of Stephen (Acts 8:1–4; 11:19). The persecutors of these Jewish believers were other non-believing Jews as well as a few Gentile neighbours (family and friends had become foes), therefore a reference to Rome as a source of persecution would seem out of place. Jerusalem is a fitting representation of those who are oppressing the recipients of this letter. Also, if 1 Peter was written prior to the destruction of Jerusalem in AD 70, which I firmly believe (see Leithart's defence of Petrine authorship in *The Promise of His Appearing*, 7), then Peter could not have meant his readers to interpret his cryptic reference as the city of Rome. The "figurative identification of Rome as Babylon is widely attested to in Israelite and Christian literature *composed **after** the Roman conquest of Judea and destruction of Jerusalem in 70 CE*," Elliot, *1 Peter*, 883. Italics and bold mine.

See also, Goppelt, *Commentary on 1 Peter*, 374. "In Jewish literature it (Babylon) was first used as a symbolic name for Rome after A.D. 70; the reason was clearly the second destruction of Jerusalem."

And Senior and Harrington, *1 Peter, Jude, and 2 Peter*, 6: "The letter probably originated at Rome, which in both Jewish and Christian literature *after 70 C.E.* was sometimes called 'Babylon' (see commentary on 5:13), particularly because of its repression of the Jewish revolt in 66–70 C.E., and the resulting destruction of Jerusalem and its Temple." (Italics mine).

description of their wickedness, and that he and his disciples had become the new Jerusalem.[11]

"And then also add Mark's name . . . my son in the faith."

Mark beamed, "Thank you, Peter. That is very gracious of you . . . in many ways I do feel like your son. You have brought me up in the faith . . . in that respect, you are my father."

"We also ought to encourage them to greet each other as well . . . they may be small house communities scattered over a fairly large area, but they are all one in Jesus," Perpetua said.

"True," Peter said, "write something like that would you Silas? And end with a blessing of peace to all those in Jesus. Amen."

"Amen," they all said in unison.

"Uhm, Peter," Mark ventured, "you don't think we ought to send them your sermons . . . the ones I wrote down, do you? We never did get around to completing what we started years ago when the persecution first broke out, remember? We spoke about it and compared stories . . . Matthew copied a lot I had written . . . but . . . we never actually wrote it all down as a single story. If we do that now, they will each have a reliable record of everything Jesus did . . . of who Jesus is."

"That would give them the ability to pass on the good news about salvation through Jesus," Mary added in support of her son's idea.

"That this may be written down for successive generations . . . that those yet to be born may bring praise to God."[12] Silas quoted from the Psalms.

"I think that is a marvellous idea, don't you Peter?" Perpetua said.

"Indeed," Peter agreed, "but I first need a drink of water."

Mark jumped up, "I'll get the water and the cups . . . and all your sermons!"

* * *

---

11. Wright remarks, "Here . . . is the all-important change of roles. Jerusalem has become Babylon; *Jesus and His disciples have become Jerusalem*," and, "The new Babylon was to be destroyed in an instant, and flight was the only appropriate action, the only way of salvation for *Jesus' renewed Israel*." Wright, *Jesus and the Victory of God*, 356n137; 360 (italics mine); cf. the references to "those who say they are Jews and are not" in Rev 2:9; 3:9.

See too: Leithart, *Revelation*; also D. Ragan Ewing, "Chapter 4: The Evidence for Jerusalem As the Harlot," Bible.org, 10 May 2004, https://bible.org/seriespage/chapter-4-evidence-jerusalem-harlot.

12. Psalm 102:19.

15

Capture and Release

It was midmorning, and the group was reclining at the table enjoying their morning repast. The dried fish from Galilee was especially good, as were the olives and the cheeses. "I really enjoyed revisiting your sermons, but my fingers are numb this morning from scribbling in those extra bits," Mark said yawning. "We really stayed up late, didn't we? But are you satisfied the stories are all in the right order . . . that I added what had been left out previously?"

"Yes . . . yes, Mark, I am. I must be honest; I was as surprised now as I was years ago at how thorough your notes were. You really did include everything important."

"And his Greek, spelling and grammar, his style . . . excellent!" Silas said, ruffling Mark's hair.

"Don't!" Mark pulled away from Silas. "You'll get salt in my hair . . . and I'll smell like a dried fish!" He ran his fingers through his hair while vigorously shaking his head. Then he turned back to Peter, "You don't think the transitions between stories are too weak? I mean, the word 'immediately' really does give the sense we are galloping through the story on a camel at high speed."

"No. No, it is fine as it is. In many ways, a sense of urgency is what we need. You just need to rewrite it as one story now." Peter looked over at Mark. He was still so young and yet he had matured and grown into a fine young man. "I am very proud of you, Mark. Thank you. That work will encourage many people. When you rewrite it, I will help you . . . we need to work on the ending a bit . . . I feel it is too abrupt. And we will need to make more copies so that it can circulate among the house communities. But it is a very fine summary of all Jesus did and taught, I think. Well done."

"I . . . well, they are all your stories . . . I just wrote down what you said," Mark protested. "I would take all those scraps of parchment home to rewrite them. Do you remember, mother?"

Mary nodded, "Only too well. You used about as much oil in the lamps as you did last night!" she teased.

"I'm sorry, mother," Mark said blushing.

* * *

"Barnabas! Saul! What brings you to Jerusalem?"

"Peter," Barnabas said, leaning into Peter's welcome embrace. "May I introduce you to our good friend from Antioch? Titus, this is one of the pillars of the community." Barnabas had his hand on the shoulder of a young man who looked Greek.

"It is an honour to finally meet you," Titus said enthusiastically. "Barnabas and Saul have told me so much about you."

"Titus," Peter echoed as he embraced him and then Saul, kissing them on both cheeks as was customary. "You are all very welcome. But, Barnabas, you still haven't answered my question. What brings you all to Jerusalem?"

"We bring gifts," Barnabas replied.

"Gifts?"

"Yes. Gifts. Of food."

"Food? I don't understand."

"You know Agabus, don't you?"

"The prophet?"

"The same, yes. While he was with us in Antioch, he predicted that there will be a famine that will spread over the whole Roman empire. So, our community in Antioch decided to provide help for our brethren in Judea."

"That is so kind . . . and so generous. Thank you. And you are both in time for the Feast of Unleavened Bread!" He looked nervously at Titus then back at Barnabas who did not seem to notice Peter's uneasiness.

"We could not have planned it better, no? But there are more sacks of food outside. If we can just get a few young men to help us unload."

"Certainly, certainly!" Turning to face the home of Mary, Peter called, "Mark?"

Mark stuck his head out of the window and looked down at the men gathered in the courtyard, "Yes, Peter? Oh! Barnabas! Saul! Hello!"

"Mark, this young man is our good friend Titus, from Antioch," Barnabas said, squinting into the bright light.

"Welcome, Titus," Mark waved.

The visitors from Antioch waved back in greeting.

"The Lord's peace be with you, young man," Barnabas said smiling.

"And also with you!" Mark replied. "I'm sorry, excuse me. What was it you wanted Peter?"

"Won't you please round up a few able-bodied young men to help Barnabas, Saul and Titus unload?"

"I will. Right away!" Mark bounded out of the room and down the stairs. He hugged the travellers, kissing them on both cheeks, before rushing out the gate and into the street.

"An impressive young man," Saul said, speaking for the first time. "Is he always this eager to help?"

"He is. All too eager at times," Peter joked.

"That's my cousin," Barnabas said laughing.

"But he is a serious young man," Peter added, "always willing to learn. You know, he was the only one I taught who actually took notes."

"Really?" Saul looked at Barnabas, "Sounds like he might be an asset to our community in Antioch. Do you think he would be up for such an adventure?"

"I don't see why not. He is a bit of a sensitive young man . . . but mature enough, I should think."

"Oh, I will take him under my wing and keep him out of harm's way," Barnabas said in an overly dramatic voice.

"Only after you have spoken with Mary," Peter reminded him. "They are very close."

"Yes . . . I will not do anything without her permission. We cannot risk losing her friendship now, can we? After all, I do need a pillow to rest my head on when I come to Jerusalem!"

"Talking about speaking with Mary, we need to see where she wants us to store these provisions. Come, let's go and find her."

They walked down to the lower part of the courtyard where the kitchen and storerooms were located looking for Mary.

"She went to the market," Rhoda informed them. "But Peter," she took him aside and whispered in his ear, "I don't know if we have enough space for what they have brought."

Peter peered out of the gate. There were a number of donkeys waiting patiently to be unburdened of their heavy cargo – bulging sacks filled with grain, dried fruits, and nuts. He imagined that this was what it looked like when Joseph sent aid to his father, first with his ten, then later his eleven, brothers during the famine. Then he saw Mary, elbowing her way up the street past the beasts of burden, and called out to her. Mark and a number of his young friends came running up behind her, talking excitedly.

"What on earth is going on?" Mary asked, slightly out of breath, "I leave my home for a short while and . . . Barnabas!" Mary raced up to him and the two cousins embraced and kissed each other several times on each cheek. "What brings you to Jerusalem? Oh, and welcome Saul . . . we were not expecting you."

"Cousin," Barnabas said affectionately, "may I introduce our friend, Titus? He came up with us from Antioch."

Mary nodded in greeting, smiling uncertainly. Titus did not look Jewish to her, and she wasn't sure of how to greet him appropriately. She looked back up at her cousin enquiringly.

"Well, the short story is that a prophet named Agabus predicted that there would be a famine . . . so we have brought enough supplies for you all."

"Oh, how kind!" Mary exclaimed, clapping her hands, and then wringing them together as she wondered where they would store such a large amount of food.

"Mother, I think we can have some of the food stored at the other homes where our brethren meet regularly," Mark offered, sensing his mother's distress.

"Indeed! Why don't we divide everything equally among the various groups in Jerusalem?" Peter said. "That way we will not have to burden anyone unnecessarily with food storage in the present and food distribution in the future."

"That's a wonderful idea," Barnabas agreed. "Mark, would you and your friends help me to locate all these homes? Then we don't have to unload everything here and then redistribute later."

"I would love to," Mark replied, "but allow us to first help unload here."

"Besides, that will give me time to talk to you about—" Barnabas looked at Peter and then at Mary.

"Talk to him about what?" Mary said, with a frown. "What are you all plotting behind my back?"

"They, that is Barnabas and Saul, were wondering if Mark might like to go with them to Antioch," Peter said, preferring to get to the point.

"Oh! May I mother? Please?" Mark pleaded, putting down a heavy sack of grain and looking at her with the most pitiful look he could muster.

Mary looked at Barnabas and then at Saul and then at Peter. Was she ready to let her son go to a place she had never been herself? Was *he* ready? She knew she couldn't keep him at home forever, but this was so sudden . . . so unexpected. She thought back of how she felt during the conversation the day before and her reaction to the thought of Mark going to Rome with Peter. The wringing of her hands intensified . . . her palms felt sweaty, and she was aware that her heart was beating rapidly.

"Give me time to think . . . to pray about this," she said finally.

"That is the least we can do," Peter began to say, but Mary had walked away giving Rhoda instructions of where to store the sacks of food.

"That's what Mother always does when she's nervous," Mark said, lifting the sack up again. "She begins to work, work, work. She says it helps her think clearly."

"She loves you dearly," Barnabas said.

"And I love her . . . it hasn't been easy . . . her raising me on her own."

"But from what I can see, she has done a good job," Saul said, ruffling Mark's hair.

"Don't . . . please," Mark protested, nearly dropping the sack.

"Ah, the burden of being born with such ruffable hair!" Peter said. They all laughed. And yet Peter wondered if this seemingly innocent and yet patronising gesture exposed an underlying prejudice . . . as if Saul viewed Mark as little more than an immature young man. Peter had checked himself earlier when he realised his own error. He had come to appreciate the maturity of his young protégé, but could others see what he saw? Could Saul see what he saw? Suddenly Peter felt protective. He decided to address the issue in private with Saul.

"I tell you what," Peter said, breaking away from his troubled thoughts, "let us unload what we will store here, and then Saul and I can pack it away, while you, Barnabas and Titus take the rest to the other homes, yes?"

"That's fine with me," Saul said. "Our last chat was cut short, Peter. This will give us some time to catch up properly."

As Mark and Barnabas walked out the gate, Peter turned to Saul and said, "And . . . perhaps you can reassure Mary while you're at it. She hardly knows you . . . and to send her son with you . . . well, that's hard for any mother."

Saul smiled. He thought about the time his parents sent him away from Tarsus to Jerusalem to study under the great Gamaliel. His mother shed copious tears while all he could think of at the time was the sense of adventure. How he wished he had been more sensitive and affectionate.

"I will do my best to assure her that I will take good care of her son," Saul said.

"Will you?" Peter asked, looking Saul in the eyes.

"What do you mean? Do you doubt me?"

"I noticed how you ruffled Mark's hair . . ."

"Seriously? And this makes you think I will not take care of him?"

"No, it just makes me wonder if you realise that he is not a child . . . it makes me wonder if you see his deep desire to serve our Lord . . . if you see his maturity."

Saul paused for a moment and then stated flatly, "He is a young man and as a young man he has much to learn. Life away from his mother is going to be difficult. Do not expect me to mother him or to be his nurse maid."

Peter did not reply, but in his heart, he wondered if this idea of Mark going with the two older men to Antioch was wise.

"Besides," Saul said matter of factly, "Mark has his cousin Barnabas with him. He will have a wing to crawl under if he needs one. Now, shall we?"

"Yes," Peter said, trying to suppress his reservations, "the sooner we get it done the sooner we can sit and catch up, right?"

* * *

"But is Titus circumcised?" Peter asked Saul under his breath as they set down the last sack of grain.

"No, he is not," Saul replied. "Does it matter? I thought that what happened in Caesarea Maritima settled that in your mind."

"In my mind, yes, but there are some here who do not agree with me. I do not wish to offend your friend."

"A fellow follower of Jesus," Saul corrected him.

"Indeed. But Saul, some of our brethren here will refuse to eat with him. Besides, this is putting Mary in a tight spot too. Is he to sleep here?"

"Could we at least talk about it?" Saul asked, clearly annoyed.

Peter sighed deeply. "Yes, I think we must. I will send Mark to find James . . . you know the brother of Jesus?"

"Yes, I know him," Saul said coolly.

"We can meet in private . . . a smaller group would be better for the time being."

* * *

"But Saul," James, the brother of Jesus said, "some brethren already know that Titus is uncircumcised. They saw you when you, if you will pardon me, relieved yourself."

"They spied on us?" Saul said, his ears turning crimson.

"No," John said uncertainly, "they just . . . well, they just happened to see. . ."

"They spied on us!" Saul hissed. "And now they think they can rob us of the freedom we have in Christ Jesus! You did not insist that Cornelius be circumcised, Peter, did you?"

"No," Peter said slowly, turning to look at James. "And I was criticised for it."

"You were criticised for eating with them," James corrected him.

"Because they were uncircumcised," Peter said defensively. "They were already God-fearers. The problem you and the others had at the time was that they had not become Jews first."

James looked away. "You are right, Peter. You are right. And here we are again, facing the same issue."

A sound of angry voices could be heard coming from the Temple area. John glanced at the window nervously. Where was his brother, James?

"You know there will always be some in our ranks who will struggle with this, Saul," Peter said facing their three visitors, "and we cannot judge those who do not understand that the old barriers have been removed through Jesus. God has accepted us all as we are, and so we need not place stumbling blocks before anyone, Jew or Gentile. We must all bear with the deficiencies of both."

"Those Gentiles who embraced Judaism and accepted all that was required of them then prior to following the Way, seem to struggle the most of all," John said softly, still distracted by the sound from outside. "They seem to be more aggressive in this matter than the rest of us."

"But that does not mean we have to be pressurised into compromise!" Saul nearly shouted.

"Lower your voice!" Barnabas fretted. "We don't need the neighbours to hear our discussion. Remember, we will be leaving soon, but Mary has to live here."

"Uhm, brothers, would it be better for me to leave?" Titus spoke for the first time. "I do not wish to be the cause of any unpleasantness or contention."

"No," James said immediately. "No, you do not need to go anywhere. You are as welcome here as our Lord Jesus himself."

"And I wish to agree with James." Mary had come to offer them refreshments and she had heard the angry exchange. She quickly walked over to where the group was standing, folding and unfolding her hands. Her lips were pressed firmly together, and her cheeks were slightly flushed. She was clearly nervous as traditionally it was not a woman's place to address men.

"This is my home," she said in a shaky voice, "and I may welcome whomever I choose."

Turning to the young Greek she added, "Titus, if my cousin says you are a brother, that is good enough for me, and ought to be good enough for everyone who claims to follow the one who loved and accepted those others rejected . . . not just the lepers and the lame and the unclean, but also the Samaritans and the Gentiles."

Mary looked around at the group. "Have you all forgotten what you taught us? Do you remember your trips to Samaria, to Phoenicia, and to the Decapolis?"

John could not look at Mary at first. He was thinking about the time he and his brother wanted to call down fire on a Samaritan village. And then there was that awful incident with the Canaanite woman and her demon possessed daughter. Jesus had rebuked them at the time and now he was rebuking them through the voice of Mary.

Saul was the first to break the awkward silence. "That was very brave of you, Mary, and I, for one, am grateful for your admonishment."

"Brethren," James said, clearing his throat, "I believe God already made his will clear to us when he poured out his Spirit on the Samaritans and then later, on the Gentile family of Cornelius."

"Amen," Peter said. "So, we need not debate this any further."

"However," John interjected, trying to be more focused. "I do believe we need to be gentle with those who disagree. After all, we are called to love first and foremost."

"Gentle, and yet firm," James said, extending his hand toward Titus who gladly accepted it. "Titus, we welcome you as a brother." He drew Titus into an embrace and kissed him on both cheeks. "We do not require anything more from you other than that you follow our Lord in holiness and integrity."

"Saul," Peter said, "I believe you are truly called to proclaim the message of Christ to the Gentiles. I must admit I feel more comfortable serving our fellow Jews, but that may be because I was not raised outside the borders of Israel. God has gifted you to speak to the Gentiles and I believe I speak for all of us when I say that you have our blessing."

John moved closer to the window to see if he could locate the origin of the shouting. Did no one else hear the noise?

"Blessed are you, Lord God," James prayed, arms stretched out, palms facing upwards as if in anticipation of a gift, "King of the Universe. You, Lord Jesus, have all authority in both heaven and earth, and you have instructed us to bring your blessing to bear upon all, even to the ends of the earth. You bestow good things on all, the righteous and the unworthy. Blessed are you, Lord God, as you are a just judge who is good and does good. Blessed are You, Lord, our God, as you have granted us all, Jew and Gentile alike . . . you have granted us eternal life, you have sustained us, and you have enabled us to reach this decision this day. Knit us together as your one body in the same way you knitted our bodies together in our mother's womb. Amen."

"Amen," the group agreed.

Peter began to sing a Psalm. "How good and how pleasing it is when brethren live together in unity."

The others joined in. "It is like the precious oil that ran down on the beard . . . even the beard of Aaron, trickling down to the collar of his robes. It is like the dew of Hermon that falls on the mountains of Zion. Here the Lord has ordained blessings, even life eternal. Amen."

Tears ran down their cheeks as the gravity of the moment sank into their consciousness. This was a day that would surely be remembered by generations to come. They stood in silence for a while, not wanting the moment to pass too quickly.

The angry shouting was getting even louder. What was happening in the city?

Mary cleared her throat. "May I ask Mark to bring up the refreshments, now?"

Barnabas beamed at her. She was the most excellent hostess. "Yes, dear cousin," he said, "and I will help. They left the room in silence.

"I would ask one thing of you, brother Saul," James said, putting his arm over Saul's shoulder and taking him to one side.

"If I am able to grant it, I will," Saul replied.

"I only ask that you remember our poor."

"But of course. As you can see, we are all too eager to do so."

"Yes, and we are grateful for your gifts of food. As you know, many of our poorer brethren have been excommunicated from the synagogues and they no longer have access to the gifts from the Temple. It is even difficult to buy food in the market for some of us. I suspect it is different for you in the diaspora?"

"It is," Titus said, having followed them. "Even the Gentile poor who relied on food offered in the pagan temples are taken care of by our group. Most people don't care what you believe as long as you do not cause trouble."

Barnabas and John Mark entered the room carrying trays filled with an assortment of eatables. Mary followed with a large jug of water.

"Mark is going to the market to buy a few more things," Mary said. "Is there anything else you think you might need? Paul, Barnabas, Titus?"

Titus smiled a broad smile. He knew Mary was wondering whether her fare was acceptable for someone used to a very different diet.

"This is more than sufficient, Mary," Barnabas answered. "Nevertheless, if you wish for us to get something more, I will go with Mark." He raised his arm and indicated to John Mark that they should go. Perhaps he could chat with him privately about the possibility of his coming with them to Antioch.

The sound of shouting was obvious to all now. John looked at Peter.

"I wonder what is happening out there," Peter said, as if to himself. Then, addressing Barnabas and Mark as they were about to leave the room, he added, "while you two are in the marketplace, find out what that commotion is all about . . . it sounds like the shouting is coming from the Temple area."

* * *

Barnabas and Mark rushed up the stairs and burst into the room. Mark's face was flushed.

"The commotion . . . the shouting . . . Herod Agrippa . . . his soldiers . . . they have arrested a number of our brethren . . . and . . . and . . ."

"And what?" Peter asked, alarmed, not meaning to look at Saul, but locking eyes with him briefly, nonetheless.

"It is James . . . John, your brother . . ." Barnabas said between deep gasps of breath.

"What about James?" John said alarmed, his face suddenly white. "Tell us!"

"Herod has . . . Herod has had him beheaded," Mark said, suddenly dissolving into tears.

* * *

"There was nothing you could have done to prevent this, Peter," Perpetua said, gently rubbing his temples.

"John is shattered. The two of them were so close . . . the sons of thunder, Jesus called them. You know, even as boys they were inseparable. They were more like best friends than brothers . . . not unlike Andrew and me."

"Has John left for Capernaum yet?"

"Yes. I can't even think of how Zebedee and Salome will react to this news . . . it will be such a shock. Imagine if it was our Petronilla who had been executed . . . or even Andrew . . ."

"I know. I've been thinking about that all day. Perhaps I should have gone with John."

"I had considered that . . . but more for your safety, I must confess."

"My safety? You don't think . . ."

"I do. This may be the beginning of another wave of persecution."

"I saw you glance at Saul earlier. He looked rather uncomfortable."

"Yes, that was unfortunate. I did not mean to . . ."

"I remember when he returned from Damascus after three years. Three years . . . and still no one trusted him."

"Yes. Yes, I remember that too. I still feel a bit guilty about that. You know, if it wasn't for Barnabas, it would have taken a lot longer for us to make contact with him. Not that I blame Nicanor or Procurus, or anyone else for that matter. They not only witnessed the stoning of Stephen, but their families suffered terribly too. Fear often breeds an inability to trust. But . . . something tells me that there is a difference between the two persecutions. I think that what happened today is a civil persecution more than a religious one. Herod just wants to win favour with the Jews."

"But why now . . . during the Feast of Unleavened Bread? What can he possibly seek to gain by killing James?"

"Many of our fellow Jews want us dead, Perpetua . . . you know that. They rejected Jesus, they had him executed unlawfully . . . and we are a constant reminder of that to them. We are an irritant."

"Not only that, but they do not like to be constantly reminded that unless they change their ways, Jesus said he would come again to judge them . . . you force them to remember what he said."

"Yes. I recall being so confused when he first said that . . . how little I understood back then. I remember he was denouncing the Pharisees and Scribes at the time . . . he called them snakes. Oh, they were so angry." Peter sucked in his breath as he recalled the look of volcanic fury on the faces of their leaders, "But then I also remember him saying that they would persecute his messengers . . . that they would kill them and crucify them and flog them in their synagogues. And that is exactly what they have done and are doing. But then," he paused, mid-sentence, frowning as he recalled the difficult sayings of Jesus, "then he added that he would avenge the blood of all the righteous shed in the land, from Abel to the present day.[1] That he would come to destroy Jerusalem and the temple in this generation."[2]

"That's what you all repeat often in your sermons . . . and I think that's why they stoned Stephen."

"From what I've been told, in his defence before the Sanhedrin, Stephen did more than that. By selectively taking them through the Scriptures, he compared our current leaders to our forefathers who hated the prophets for the same reasons they hate Jesus and us. Oh, Perpetua," Peter turned to face his wife with a look of sorrow on his face. "Their religion is so empty . . . they have a form, but no content. You know, I've never understood what makes people hold to institutional systems and customs while rejecting the reality behind the forms. How can they even call themselves Jews while they play these political games with the Romans? In the name of the law, they break the law."

---

1. Matthew 23:33–39.
2. Matthew 24:2; Luke 19:41–44.

Perpetua cupped her husband's face in her hands and looked deeply into his trouble eyes, "For them it's not about God anymore, Peter. You know that. It is all about power and status."

"And power and status corrupt even the best of us."

"Oh, Peter, may God spare us from that! It will be a sad day when power and status rear their ugly heads in our community."

Peter turned his head and stared into the darkness, "Yes. That is why it is imperative for us to instil the character of Jesus in every one of our disciples. He stayed humble, even though he was among us as the Son of God, our Master and our Lord . . . he never abused his power. He was always first and foremost a servant."

"That is because he always sought to do God's will above all else."

"Yes, even to death on the cross . . . never a thought for himself."

"Do you really think so?" Perpetua moved to once more face Peter, "I mean, do you really think that Jesus never thought about his own safety . . . his own comfort? You don't think he struggled with being obedient through suffering?"

"I think he struggled with many things, my dear wife," Peter said, taking her hand in his and returning her gaze. "Remember, in his flesh, he was a human just like us, and he was surely tempted in every way we are tempted[3] . . . but I think that where the difference comes in, is that his mind was so set on doing the will of the Father that, even during the times of struggle, he would immediately submit to that will."

Peter sighed. He was thinking about Jesus's prayer in the Garden, that night when none of them . . . Peter, John . . . yes, not even James himself . . . none of them could stay awake to pray with Jesus, even though they all knew he was in such distress. There was an intense struggle going on in his heart that night, Jesus knew what he was about to suffer . . . but in spite of the horror, he surrendered to what he knew was right. For the sake of them, and all those who would believe, he chose to endure the shame and pain of the cross.[4] What would he have done now, if he was in Peter's place? Would he hide?

"Peter?"

"Yes, my dear?"

"Promise me you won't go looking for trouble."

Peter sighed again. She always seemed to have the uncanny ability to read his thoughts, "I will not go looking for it, Perpetua, but if it comes my way, I

---

3. Hebrews 4:15.

4. Philippians 2:5–8; Hebrews 5:7–8; 12:2.

will face it. We cannot hide forever. We have the light . . . we need to shine it in their darkness."

"Even if it means?"

"Even if it means being executed, yes."

Perpetua was silent for a moment. Then she said, "You are right. We cannot hide forever . . . we cannot hide the light from the world. It is our privilege and our duty to share it. Indeed, it would be shameful for us to hide the light. But, remember, Jesus said we must be wise as serpents."

"Do not think that I desire persecution, Perpetua. I do not. I am not brave—"

"Peter—"

"Nor am I reckless."

"No . . . and you are not stupid, either. I only ask that you exercise caution. You are perceived to be a pillar of our community . . . you will be a target."

* * *

"Oh, dear Lord," Peter prayed silently, "how did this happen? How is it that I am now back in this prison cell?"

Peter had left Mary's home at dusk, hoping that the poor visibility of that hour would act as a cloak for his movements. He had been careful, as he promised Perpetua, but he wanted to find out more about the execution of James . . . and whether or not they ought to be worried that this persecution might increase and spread. The soldiers seemed to have come out of nowhere. Before he could turn to run, they had grabbed him and dragged him off to prison. How did they even know where to find him? Were they looking for him? Did someone betray him as Judas betrayed Jesus? Surely not. No. That was not possible. Fear often breeds an inability to trust, he had said. He must not allow that to happen with him.

Peter was chained to two sweaty Roman guards, both of whom were asleep on either side of him, snoring loudly. They were rough and cruel young men. Their language and topic of conversation was not edifying at all. But Peter was concerned for them. They had no hope and no purpose. He had told them about Jesus. They had cursed him in return. Although later, one of them, the one named Atticus, seemed to be interested, but he appeared to be overly concerned for the opinion of his fellow soldier. Desire for the respect of others could be such a powerful thing.

Peter thought back to the time when Jesus had told him that one day, he would face death by execution. Would he be beheaded in the morning, just like James? He had always thought that he would be crucified, and he had already decided that he would request to be crucified upside down as he was not worthy of dying in the same way as his Lord. He wondered what it was like to be killed. Was it painful? He remembered Jesus screaming out in pain on the cross. Was it quick? No, he thought. It took hours to die . . . unless it was death by beheading. Perhaps that was instant. But then, would he be afraid? Would his fear show and betray a lack of faith and trust? Jesus had told them not to be anxious, that he would be with them, that they would be given the words to speak . . . would he be given courage too?

He must have nodded off as he woke up with a start. There was a blinding light shining in his cell. He looked up and saw a large being standing before him. "I'm dreaming," he thought, "or is this another angel? Like the last time . . . but I was awake the last time . . ."

"Get up quickly," the being said.

Peter felt the chains slip off his wrists. He glanced over at his two captors. They were still fast asleep.

"Get dressed and put on your sandals. Wrap your cloak around you and follow me," the being said. The guards had stripped him earlier, sniggering, mocking him, and humiliating him with all manner of filthy and lewd remarks. They told him that it was to prevent him from running away . . . that in the unlikely event he managed to free himself, he would be less inclined to escape naked. But he felt it was just to humiliate him . . . for them to have some fun at his expense.

The being began to move toward the door and Peter followed him, "This is such a vivid and real dream," Peter thought, "everything seems so real."

They passed the first and second sentries . . . the men were awake, but they did not seem to see the being or Peter. The iron gate that led to the city simply opened before them and they walked out into the streets of Jerusalem. For a short while, the being was with him and then suddenly, he was gone.

The street was dark and silent. Peter felt for the walls of the building next to him. The coolness of the stones brought him to his senses. This was no dream. God had sent an angel to deliver him!

Silently, he made his way back to the house of Mary. He knocked quietly at the gate. He could hear muted voices . . . it sounded like people praying inside.

"Who is it?" Rhoda whispered.

"Rhoda, it is me, Peter. Open the gate."

Rhoda made a squeaking sound and then ran off. He could hear her telling someone inside that Peter was standing at the gate . . . but they seemed not to believe her.

He knocked again.

More hushed arguing voices. "What is wrong with them?" he thought, "Don't they know God is able to answer even the most impossible prayer if he so wills?"

He knocked a little louder. He heard hurried footsteps approaching on the other side.

The gate flew open, "Peter!" Perpetua threw her arms around him and drew him in. Rhoda quickly closed the gate.

"Shh . . . keep your voices down," Peter said.

"We heard you had been taken prisoner," Perpetua whispered, still holding onto her beloved husband. "Oh, you're bleeding. Your wrists . . . what did they do to you."

"The chains must have chafed and broken my skin. But come, let us go inside. I will tell you what happened."

Once inside Peter said, "It is true. I was in prison. I was chained between two Roman guards. Locked inside with sentries at every entrance. But God sent an angel . . ." He continued to tell them about his miraculous deliverance.

Perpetua bathed and bandaged his wrists as he spoke.

"Peter," Mary said, "they will be looking for you, come morning light."

"Yes, you need to leave . . . now," Saul said.

"I will pack our things quickly," Perpetua said as she left the room.

"Barnabas," Peter said, "you must tell James[5] and the others about this. They will need to care for our community without me."

"I will tell him. But you must be quick. Before they post soldiers at the gates."

"And Barnabas . . . there is this young soldier by the name of Atticus," Peter said, his hand on his friend's arm, "I told him about Jesus. He seemed receptive . . . please . . ."

"I will see if I can contact him in any way, although it will be difficult."

"Pray for him, too, please. A lost lamb if ever there was one. You know how to get in contact with me . . . I will go from here to Caesarea and then on to Antioch. Please, you all must stay safe. You will be in our prayers."

"I am ready," Perpetua said.

"So quick?" Mary said.

"Well, I thought perhaps we might have to leave in haste, so I packed most of our belongings earlier. Besides, we don't have much. We have learned over the years to travel light."

---

5. This would be James, the brother of Jesus. There is a transition of leadership here, from the apostles to postapostolic leaders.

"Come," Peter said, wrapping his arm protectively around his wife, "you are my most precious possession."

"And you are mine," she responded with a swift kiss on his cheek.

"The Lord go with you and protect you!" Mary whispered.

"And the Lord be with you, dear friend," Perpetua whispered back.

They hurried out into the dark streets.

"Peter," Perpetua said softly, "we are not running and hiding . . . this is what God wills."

"Yes," he whispered back, "it would seem so. He weaves together even the misdeeds of others to create his master plans!"

* * *

16

Return to Rome

"Peter," Philip said as he entered the room, "Herod is in town."

"Why? What is he doing here?" Perpetua said, concerned. "Surely he cannot know we are here in Caesarea?"

"No, he is here to meet with a delegation from Tyre and Sidon," Philip replied. "Apparently, he has been here for some time, so if he came here looking for you, we would have known that by now. Still, there are many soldiers around. I think we need to be extra careful."

"Where is he now?" Peter asked.

"I've been told he is going to the Roman amphitheatre to address the crowds."

"Is there a way we can get close to watch?"

"Peter . . . now what did I say about you looking for trouble?" Perpetua protested.

"I'm not looking for trouble. I would just like to know what is going on . . . for our own peace of mind."

"I suppose we could try," Philip said. "Here, put on my cloak. If you see soldiers, just cover your face. I'm sure we will be able to blend in pretty easily. We can approach the amphitheatre from the opposite end . . . that way we will avoid all those soldiers stationed around Herod's palace. As far as I know there is nothing going on at the hippodrome, but still . . . I would prefer avoiding that area altogether."

"I'm coming with you," Perpetua said.

"No, my love . . ."

"Peter. I'm not going to debate this with you. It is better that we both be taken at the same time than for me to be alone as a widow for the rest of my life."

"That's a little melodramatic, don't you think? I'm not going to be arrested."

"I don't know that. You don't know that. We are one, remember . . . we've been through this before."

Philip cleared his throat, "I'm still here, remember?"

"Ah, there's no arguing with Perpetua once she has made up her mind," Peter joked, "but you need something to cover your face as well."

"I have my own cloak, thank you." She smiled and then touched his arm tenderly, "I'm not trying to be difficult, Peter."

"Perhaps it is for the best," Philip offered, "because you, Peter, will be more careful with Perpetua around than if you were on your own."

"You see?" Perpetua teased, "Even Philip can see reason."

"I know when I am beaten," Peter said, chuckling. "Come, let us go."

Thankfully, the theatre was close to the shoreline, so there was a gentle cool breeze that blew from the sea. Their cloaks were quite appropriate.

"I remember the first time we visited here . . . to speak with Cornelius. I remember thinking that this was one of the most beautiful cities I'd ever seen," Peter whispered as they walked toward the place where Herod had gathered the people together.

"There are many beautiful buildings here, yes, but I still don't like those colossal statues of the Roman imperial family at the entrance of the harbour," Perpetua whispered back. "I think that they are idolatrous, especially since the Caesars see themselves as divine."

"Many of the buildings were dedicated to Augustus," Philip added. "There's an inscription that you might find interesting . . ."

"You mean the one mentioning Pontius Pilate's dedication of the temple to Tiberius?" Peter asked.

"So you've seen it?"

"Yes, Cornelius showed us many things when we were here."

"Of course . . ."

"Soldiers, Peter!" Perpetua whispered.

"Yes, my love . . . I see them. Just act normal . . . don't draw attention to yourself."

It soon became clear that the soldiers were not looking for them . . . it seemed they were more interested in finding something alcoholic to drink.

"At this time of day?" Perpetua remarked.

"They are not employed for their morals, Perpetua," Philip said. "In fact, I've been told that they are often employed precisely because they are coarse and immoral. That way, they are not overly bothered by a conscience. Theirs is a bloody work."

"And there's the theatre," Peter indicated the high brown stone walls looming up just ahead of them.

"So many people thronging . . . we will easily blend in, Peter," Perpetua said, finally relaxing.

They navigated their way through the thickest parts of the crowd, making sure they were well hidden in the middle of bundles of people.

"Come . . . through here," Philip said, indicating a door furthest away from the stage.

They entered the huge circular, open-air structure along with a crowd of Sidonians. Perpetua uncovered her face so that she could safely navigate the stairs leading upward. She glanced up as she took her first step and thought it appeared as if the climb would lift her into the sky itself. A wave of dizziness made her pause for a moment and she felt the impatient shoulders and elbows of those behind her pushing her forward and upward. She reached out and took Peter's hand to steady herself. Hundreds of seagulls flew overhead, screeching loudly in anticipation of any waste left by the crowds of people. After what felt like an age, they found a place to sit near the very top in the shadow of one of the walls.

Suddenly there were trumpets and the crowd rose as one, cheering as Herod swept into the theatre dressed in a glittering silver robe. The morning sun's rays illuminated each sparkling strand in the cloak, giving Herod an otherworldly appearance, as if he were radiating light from within himself. Perhaps that is what he had intended, as soon the people began to cry out that he was a god and not a man. This chant was taken up by more and more people as Herod began to deliver his speech.

"This is blasphemy, Peter," Perpetua said under her breath, "he ought to rebuke them!"

Peter noticed that an owl had perched on a rope just above Herod's head . . . this seemed to bother the king . . . perhaps he thought it was a bad omen.[1] Herod suddenly grabbed his abdomen and bent over double as if in severe pain. A collective gasp came from the crowd. Then he appeared to recover and stood up straight once more. Beads of sweat glistened on his forehead and upper lip, adding a strange sparkle to his face. Suddenly he lurched to one side, grabbing at his midriff with claw like hands, as if trying to tear out his bowels. He fell to his knees, roaring in agony. Those around him rushed to his side and carried him out to the palace. The crowd panicked, some running, other jumping down the stairs, streaming out of the theatre while crying and beating

---

1. Josephus, *Antiquities*, 19.8.

their breasts. Philip, Peter, and Perpetua were at the back of the crowds, so they were not pushed in the direction of the palace . . . and once outside, they simply turned right and walked home.

* * *

"The king has died . . . apparently he died sometime during the night. They say he was infested with worms," Philip informed them.

"Worms?" Perpetua grimaced.

"What an awful way to die," Peter said, "I would not wish that on my worst enemy . . . which, I suppose, he was in some sense."

"I think you ought to take advantage of the chaos and flee to Antioch," Philip said.

"What? Are you trying to get rid of us?" Peter joked.

"Do I really need to answer that? You know how we love you."

"And we love you . . . and, as always, you are right. This would be a good time for us to leave."

"Should we venture out to see how things are at present?" Perpetua suggested. "If things do not look safe, we could return to leave another day perhaps?"

"Are you ready to leave?" Peter asked amazed.

"Peter, our daughter is in Rome . . . have you forgotten? I am longing to see her."

"We could go by sea, if you like."

"No. No, I know you want to visit all the communities along the way. And so do I. It is important that we show them they are not forgotten."

"I will walk with you as far as the road to Antioch," Philip offered. "We can skirt around the city and thus avoid the palace area altogether."

"Many Sidonians ought to be returning home . . . we could walk with them," Peter suggested.

"There will be many people walking on the road . . . given the current events, no one will be looking for you," Philip assured them.

The family joined hands and offered up prayers for a safe journey. Philip's daughters had a way of weaving into their prayers the great promises of God, that served to remind them that, regardless of the outcome of this journey, a good God was with them all the way . . . like a good shepherd.

Leaving the compound, they found that the city was strangely quiet. It was as if the death of the king had muted all sound out of the streets. Even in the marketplace, transactions were completed in hushed tones. They bought some freshly baked bread and a skin of wine for the road. It would take them a few days to get to their destination, but thankfully the believers everywhere tended to be open to receiving unexpected guests. It was as if their minority status knit them together more tightly.

As expected, many Sidonians were on the road already, and the foot traffic from the south increased the volume of travellers even more. There were soldiers on the road, of course, but they seemed tense and hurried.

"God go with you, my dear friends," Philip said.

"And God be with you, too . . . with you all," Peter replied.

"You are always in our prayers, Philip," Perpetua said as she kissed him on both cheeks.

"God alone knows when we will meet again," Philip said.

Peter did not know how to respond to this last statement. Life was so fragile at the best of times, but the growing opposition from both Jewish and Gentile quarters was mounting wherever there were believers. Who knew what was waiting for them in Rome?

* * *

"Peter?" Peter looked up and saw the scrunched-up face of John Mark before him.

"Mark!" Perpetua cried, jumping up and embracing the young man, "Oh, what a happy sight . . . what a wonderful surprise! Oh, and Barnabas and Saul too!"

"This is a very unexpected blessing!" Barnabas said. "We thought you were well on your way to Rome by now."

"We stopped in Caesarea for a while . . . but after Agrippa's death we decided to move on to Antioch," Peter explained. "Am I right in thinking that is where you are headed?"

"Yes," Saul replied, "our mission in Jerusalem is now complete, so we are returning home."

"And your mother let you go with them?" Perpetua asked still holding onto Mark, successfully resisting the urge to ruffle that curly mop of dark hair.

"Barnabas had to promise to look after me," Mark said, clearly happy to be part of the group.

"It is very difficult for a parent to let their child go," Perpetua said, smiling, "I know. Leaving Petronilla in Rome was one of the hardest things I've ever done."

"What are your plans," Saul asked, "from here to Antioch and then?"

"Back to Rome via the communities in Cappadocia, Pontus, Bithynia, Galatia . . . and perhaps others along the way," Peter replied. "Wherever our Lord may lead, I suppose."

"We were talking about doing something similar . . . but going to places you have not been to yet," Saul added. "My desire is to work where no one else has worked before."

"You have a lot of places to choose from then," Peter said. "Many have not yet heard about Jesus . . . Jews and Gentiles alike. And you have a lot to offer, Saul. You are better educated than most of us and so many of our countrymen need to hear a well-reasoned defence of the gospel. I always teach my disciples to be ready to give a reason for the hope that is in them[2] . . . and you will give them the tools they need to do so."

"You are too kind, Peter . . . I'm afraid there are many who still see me for what I was, a Pharisee and a persecutor. Wherever I go I am viewed with suspicion."

"Yes, first impressions are difficult to overcome, but in time . . ."

"That is one of the reasons I want to go where I am not yet known."

"It might not be that easy, Saul. Travel is so much easier these days with these Roman roads. You may find your name has gone before you. Nevertheless, bringing light to those who live in darkness is well worth the difficulties encountered along the way. It is more rewarding than anything else I have ever done."

"And your wife?"

"Don't talk about me as if I am not here, Saul," Perpetua teased. "You want to know if I find the travelling as rewarding as my husband? Yes, I do. While it is true that no self-respecting Jewish man would listen to anything I have to say, even as a witness to what Peter teaches, the women are very ready to talk. So many of them are deeply moved when I tell them about Jesus and the way he respected and treated the women in his following. But Peter is not the only one who has a wife as travel companion. Jude, the Lord's brother, has Rachel . . . a very willing and able companion."

"Yes, I have heard. That is wonderful."

"You did not marry, Saul?" Perpetua asked.

"No. To be honest, I was so devoted to my learning that the thought never crossed my mind. I was so intent on being the best Torah student under Gamaliel that I . . . well, I didn't have time for anything else. They used to tease me and say that too much learning will make me mad one day. But now I think the learning is helping me train new converts to Jesus."

"And you are not lonely?"

---

2. 1 Peter 3:15; cf. Colossians 4:5–6.

"Not really. I have learned to be content in every situation of life. And, in one sense, I am better off as I am . . . if I was married, I may be distracted from doing the Lord's will. Married men are often concerned about worldly things . . . they worry about their wife . . . they want to please their wife. But I believe you and Peter are unique . . . you both seek the kingdom first."

"Yes, I am blessed," Peter said, drawing Perpetua closer to himself, "Perpetua does not care for the things of this world."

Saul nodded, but said nothing further.

Turning to Barnabas Peter said, "Barnabas. That young soldier, Atticus. Did you manage to talk with him at all?"

"No, I did not, unfortunately," Barnabas replied. "When they could not find you, Agrippa had all the soldiers executed."

"What?" Peter exclaimed. "Why? Oh, how terrible . . . they died because of me."

"No . . . well, yes, in a sense . . . but it may be of some comfort for you to know that those who witnessed the execution said that Atticus claimed to be a follower of Jesus and that he was telling the others what, I presume, you told him."

"Thanks be to God!" Peter exclaimed. "He is always so faithful to germinate the meagre seeds we sow!"

"A good reminder for us all that while it is our responsibility to sow, to plant, and to water, it is God alone who can change hearts or bring about growth,"[3] Saul added.

"Shall we walk together?" Barnabas asked suddenly. "There is still so much we would like to talk about, but the day is moving on and we still have a long way to go."

"And Rome is beckoning," Perpetua said. "The one earthly object I do care for, Saul . . . besides my husband, of course . . . is my daughter. And we have many stops in between."

"You are a remarkable woman, Perpetua," Saul said, smiling.

"Perhaps, one day, you will say those words to a fortunate young lady."

"Ah, Perpetua . . . ever the matchmaker!" Peter said, laughing, "Enough already. Come, let us press on."

"To Rome!" Perpetua said in an exaggerated voice.

"To Rome," Peter echoed, "and all the other cities in between."

Perpetua jabbed him in the ribs. They all laughed.

✳ ✳ ✳

---

3. 1 Corinthians 3:6.

17

Return from Rome and Delicate Deliberations

I'm afraid we left Rome under a bit of a cloud," Peter said as they gathered together in the upper room of Mary's home.

"How so?" Mark asked, without looking up.

Peter noticed that the young man seemed a little subdued, as if his usual youthful exuberance had been quenched. The light in his eyes was dull. Peter glanced at his mother, but Mary shook her head, indicating that she knew something was wrong, but that she wasn't entirely sure what.

"You remember the last time we were here, we told you about some trouble between our brethren and the Jews . . . and that there were rumours that Claudius would expel all Jews from the capital because of this? Well, we think this will happen soon. The situation is quite tense now."

"What about Petronilla?" Mary asked, alarmed.

"Oh, she is with Jude and Rachel . . . if they need to leave, they know where to go," Perpetua said, wishing she sounded more convincing than she did.

"She will be fine," Peter placed his hand over hers, "the Lord is with her."

"As he is with us, yes," she replied, unbidden tears suddenly stinging her eyes.

"What poor company we are," Peter said smiling a tender smile.

"Not poor company, no. We can see that something has happened that has brought on sadness . . . what is it? Is this about what is happening in Rome, or something else?" Silas asked, concerned.

"Not Rome, no," he looked over at Mark again. It really did seem that there was a cloud of grief hanging over him. Perhaps, now was not the time to talk about their own difficulties. "I will tell you about that later . . . let me first tell you about the journey."

Perpetua stared down at the table but said nothing.

Peter cleared his throat, "So, Rome . . . Mark, you always like to hear about our travels . . . we travelled north-east from Rome to the coast and then sailed over to Dalmatia. We decided to take the road through Thrace because we wanted to visit the communities in Bithynia and Pontus, Galatia, and Cappadocia. You remember, Mark? That strange land I told you about with those peculiar, conical-shaped hills . . . people carved out homes in them . . . do you remember?"

Mark nodded but did not speak. Peter saw that Mary was wringing her hands again as she always did when she was nervous. What had happened to rob Mark of his joy?

Peter continued, "We wanted to go via Skepsis to see Cornelius, but that would have lengthened our journey considerably. We would have had to travel south and then east . . . so it was a pity, but unavoidable."

There was an awkward pause in the conversation.

"Have you heard from him at all?" Mary asked. She was hoping to encourage Mark to ask questions, but so far, she had not succeeded in reawakening his old characteristic curiosity.

"Yes, we have. Actually, he and Clement correspond on a regular basis. The community in Skepsis is growing from strength to strength."

"And the other communities . . . the ones you visited?" Mary said, glancing once again at her sullen, silent son.

"They are doing well," Peter replied. "There are real concerns though, as opposition from our countrymen seems to be mounting there too. Some of them once professed belief in Jesus, but now they say the fact that Jerusalem still stands indicates that Jesus was either mistaken or worse a false prophet."

"Yes, we have heard that here too. 'Where is this coming you always talk about?'[1] they ask," Silas said.

"And what do you tell them?" Peter asked.

"Well," Silas replied thoughtfully, "we tell them that God is merciful and longsuffering . . . that he wants to give them enough time to repent and believe . . . that he does not wish for one sinner to perish."[2]

"That is a good answer," Peter said, "but also remember that God has his own time schedule. Jesus told us it is not for us to know times or seasons . . . the Father sets the times by his own authority."[3]

---

1. 2 Peter 3:4.

2. 2 Peter 3:9.

3. Acts 1:7; cf. 1 Thessalonians 5:1–2.

Mark suddenly looked up and said, "That is a little trite, don't you think? An easy answer for a difficult question?"

There was an uncomfortable pause as Peter thought about what the younger man had just said. There was clearly some pain in his statement. Peter suspected that it was something deeper than Mark himself had explored.

"Perhaps," Peter admitted, "but I think if you express that answer in terms of God's unchanging character, it is not quite as trite as it may seem on the surface."

"What do you mean?" Ah, the interest was not completely eclipsed.

"I mean," Peter continued, "that if one considers the fact that our God is a God of wisdom, mercy, compassion, kindness, love, grace, goodness . . . and the fact that our God is always faithful, and he is always the same, yesterday, today, and for all eternity[4] . . . that changes the way you experience the world around you, and interpret the events of life, both good and evil. If your focus is on him . . . on *who* he is . . . then you will view the circumstances of life, whether good or bad, in a very different light."

"Is it really that easy for you?" Mark asked. "I mean look at our world. What has changed for the better? People still do awful things, people are still unkind, people still live in fear, is it any wonder that I . . . that we . . . that some struggle with doubt?"

"I did not say it was easy, Mark."

"But your answer," Mark interrupted with a tinge of bitterness on his voice, "your answer is condescending . . . it is patronizing. You make people with genuine concerns sound stupid . . . as if they don't have enough faith. Your oversimplistic reply adds guilt to their doubts." Mark was flushed in the face and white, foamy spittle had collected on his lower lip.

"Mark! Do not speak to Peter like that," Mary said, her voice quivering, hands wringing.

"I must speak truth, mother, not so? That is what you always tell me."

"Yes, but you can do so respectfully . . . I'm sorry Peter."

Peter shook his head in an attempt to show Mary he was not offended. "Mark," he began, speaking softly, "you have always been like a son to us. We can see that you are hurting."

Mark breathed out loudly through his nose, "I am sorry, Peter . . . I did not mean to be disrespectful. Excuse me, I need some air." He got up suddenly and left the room. Peter thought he saw angry tears flowing down his cheeks.

"I am so sorry, Peter," Mary began.

---

4. Hebrews 13:8.

"No, please do not apologize . . . he is hurting."

"What has happened?" Perpetua asked taking Mary's hands in her own.

"I don't really know the details . . . you know he went with Barnabas and Saul to Antioch."

"We do," Peter said, "we met them along the way. Mark seemed so happy and excited."

"As he was when he left Jerusalem. But apparently, after they had been in Antioch for a while, they went to Cyprus, where Barnabas . . . or rather, where we still have family. From what I can gather, everything went well while they were on the island, but then they went to a place called Perga."

"Yes, I know where that is . . . it is on the mainland."

"I don't know . . . I've led such an insulated life. But there . . . there something happened to Mark . . . something that made him come back to Jerusalem."

"Do you have any idea?" Peter asked.

"He has not spoken about it," Silas said. "I've tried, but he has not been willing to say anything to me. It may have been some crisis of faith. He did mention something about the conversion of the proconsul of Cyprus, Sergius Paulus . . . something Paul should have done but didn't."[5]

"Whatever it was, it has left a scar on his life," Perpetua said. "Peter . . . perhaps if we share with him our own hurt?"

"That might draw him out to speak of his own," Peter said thoughtfully.

"That's what I was thinking."

"What hurt?" Mary asked.

Peter sighed, "There was something I wanted to tell you all . . . but I thought it unwise in the light of Mark's sad demeanour. Perhaps I was wrong. It is something painful."

"Painful?" Silas asked.

"Yes. Yes, it was painful at the time . . . to be honest, it still is, in a way . . . but it was and still is a good reminder that it is easy to slip back into old ways of thinking."

---

5. It is possible that Mark's abrupt departure from Perga may have been theological. According to Erbey Valdez in his book *On the Shores of Perga*, Luke's use of Mark's Hebrew name, John, only in this passage, the participle form of the verb αφισημι, meaning deliberate desertion, the fact that Mark returned to Jerusalem and not Antioch, and the immediate explosion of the Gentile controversy in the narrative, may have been intentional. It may be that Luke was trying to show that John (Mark) disagreed with Saul (Paul) on the subject of circumcision following the conversion of the Gentile proconsul of Cyprus, Sergius Paulus. Given Paul's adamant refusal to take him on the second journey we must assume Mark's departure was something more than simple homesickness.

Perpetua noticed Mark standing in the doorway. She smiled, the curiosity was still there . . . he did not want to miss anything important. He appeared to have washed his face, possibly to remove any sign of tears. She rose and gently led him back into the room.

"Will you sit with me, Mark?" She asked.

He nodded, shy now as he felt embarrassed.

"I was just about to tell them, Mark, about . . . about what is troubling us," Peter said. "I said I would tell you later, but I think now may be a good time . . . as good a time as any. After we had revisited some of the churches along the way from Rome, as I've already told you, we stopped a while longer in Antioch."

Peter paused for a moment. Perpetua reached out and held his hand in hers. Mark leaned forward as if to hear better. Was it possible that the great pillar of the community had been wounded too?

"Barnabas and Saul were there. At first all went well. But then a few of our more religiously rigid Jewish believers arrived from Jerusalem . . . those who still hold to the Jewish dietary regulations." He sighed deeply as he recalled his unfortunate behaviour and the hurt that followed. "I don't know why, but I stopped eating with the Gentile believers. You know, I never thought I would be intimidated by anyone since that awful night in the high priest's courtyard. But I guess I was wrong. What was worse, I caused Barnabas to stumble too. Saul . . . or Paul as they call him now . . . well he was so angry with us he shouted at both of us in front of everyone . . . he called us play actors, the word Jesus used for the Pharisees."[6]

"I remember that anger very well," Mark mumbled. But then he added, as if emboldened by what Peter had said, "I left Barnabas and Paul in Pamphylia because . . . well, no . . . let me not blame him. I was not ready for his changed theology . . . and he was not ready for my unreadiness."

So, that's what is bothering him, Peter thought to himself. But who was not ready, he wondered? The leader or the one being led?

"I'm sorry, Mark," he said out loud, reaching over Perpetua and placing his hand on the younger man's arm. "We leaders need to learn that not everyone is where we want them to be. I think that was a gift Jesus had . . . he always saw what we could be, not what we had been . . . nor, indeed, what we were at the time. And he also knew how to take us to where he wanted us to be . . . gently. You know, it was like he would take you on a spiritual journey, lead you down the paths he knew you needed to go, where you would learn the lessons you needed to learn."

---

6. Galatians 2:11–14.

Peter paused to reflect on what he had just said. Then he added, "To be honest, I'm not sure I have that gift. I lose patience too quickly. And that is my fault . . . not my disciple's."

"I . . . I don't know what to say, Peter," Mark said quietly. "Forgive my outburst earlier . . . I didn't mean . . . I didn't . . . well, you have always been very kind to me *and* very patient. You're the kind of person I really don't want to hurt or disappoint."

"Well . . . I disappointed myself . . . I still do . . . I still disappoint myself," Peter said. "I was weak in Antioch. Paul was right. True, I think he might have handled the situation differently . . . he might have taken us aside privately, as Jesus had taught us[7] . . . but no matter. What's done is done. And so we are here to settle the matter once and for all."

"What do you mean?" Silas asked.

Peter sat up straight once again. He looked at Perpetua and then said, "A church council is to be held here in Jerusalem. Barnabas and Paul are coming from Antioch together with a few delegates . . . we are here already. Without clear guidelines, others are going to make the same blunders I made, and the church may end up being divided over some very marginal issues. What we seek to do is what the wise king, Solomon told us to do: 'Catch us the little foxes,' he said, 'the little foxes that destroy the vineyard, for our vines have developing grapes.'[8] We need to pray . . . pray for the guidance of the Holy Spirit . . . pray for wisdom and for unity. Jesus said he would guide us in matters of truth, and so we must wait on him, and then make a decision as a united community."

"That is very sensible, I think," Silas said. "That way everyone will know what to do in the future."

"Will you address the council too?" Mary asked.

"Yes, I will. Paul was right. I thought I had learned the lesson with that vision in Caesarea. Actually, it is worse than that."

"How so?" Mark asked. Perpetua looked over at Mary, her eyes twinkling . . . sharing their own vulnerability seemed to have coaxed Mark out of his melancholy. Mary was no longer wringing her hands.

"Well, once again I was caught unawares. Not unawares . . . maybe that's the wrong word to use. Watchful. I ought to have been more watchful . . . Jesus once told me that I had the right spirit, but my mind . . . well I was not quite

---

7. Matthew 18:15–17.
8. Song of Solomon 2:15.

as strong as I thought.[9] And I failed him . . . I failed him in Jerusalem, and I failed him in Antioch."

"Peter, no!" Perpetua said. "That is too harsh."

"I agree," Mary said, suddenly moving around the table and putting her hand on Peter's shoulder. "It was a mistake. We all make mistakes, Peter, even the best of us." She looked over at her son to see his reaction. Mark was nodding and he seemed to be more at ease. Perhaps in sharing his error, Peter had indeed helped to make Mark see that he was not alone in his human frailty.

"Yes, that is why we need Jesus . . . that is why we need Jesus all the time," Peter agreed. Then looking up at Mark again, he added, "Remember what I said in the letter we wrote together the last time I was here, Mark?"

"About what? You said many things in that letter."

"About the evil one."

"Yes, I do remember. You said that we always have to be on our guard because he prowls around like a scavenger seeking to devour those who are not vigilant."[10]

"Vigilant. That's a good word. You always had a way with words."

Mark was responding well to the wisely tempered praise.

"Well, I was not vigilant . . . and my behaviour very nearly caused a split in the community in Antioch."

"But the community did not split," a voice came from the doorway. For a moment they could not identify the man as he was silhouetted by the bright sunlight outside.

"Barnabas!" Mark ran to embrace his cousin.

Clearly, Peter thought to himself, Barnabas is not the one who has wounded him.

"How good to see you!" That energetic enthusiasm that so endeared Mark to everyone who knew him seemed to have returned.

But then Mark noticed the short, bald, bow-legged man[11] standing behind his cousin. "Ah! Paul!" he said, almost choking in surprise, "you are here too." Mark backed away.

---

9. Matthew 26:41.

10. 1 Peter 5:8.

11. Two New Testament apocryphal books give a description of Paul's physical appearance. In the Acts of Paul and Thecla, Onesiphorus describes Paul as "a man small of stature, with a bald head and crooked legs, in a good state of body, with eyebrows meeting and nose somewhat hooked, full of friendliness; for now he appeared like a man, and now he had the face of an angel." In the Acts of Paul, the apostle is described as "A man of small stature, with a bald head and crooked legs, in a good state of body, with eyebrows meeting and nose somewhat hooked." See

The atmosphere suddenly changed . . . as if all the air had been sucked from the room.

"You are most welcome," Mary said, breaking the tension, but once more wringing her hands. She walked up to the travellers from Antioch, "Please, come in and make yourselves at home." She glanced at Mark who, she thought, resembled a frightened rabbit. In an attempt to rescue her son she grabbed his arm and said, "Mark, please fetch more cups and more water."

"Yes, mother," he said and fled.

Peter stood up to greet Barnabas and Paul.

"I heard part of what you were saying, Peter," Paul said stepping forward past Barnabas into the room and embracing Peter, "Perpetua is right. You are too harsh on yourself . . . and I was too harsh on you as well. I was as much in error as both of you. My rage was not warranted . . . and I should not have shamed you in public. Will you please forgive me?"

Peter paused. Why was this so difficult? Why had it taken Paul so long to admit his fault in the matter?[12] And was he himself not playing the hypocrite after all? Should he not have confronted Paul earlier rather than talk about the incident with others? And why was there this struggle in his heart? He knew that forgiveness was a choice, he had been forgiven so much he ought to forgive freely . . . surely, it was merely his wounded pride getting in the way. With a determination to overcome his emotions, Peter placed both his hands on Paul's shoulders and looked straight into his eyes.

"With all my heart, brother. I forgive you. I stand with you . . . with you both . . . on this matter of Gentile inclusion . . . as you well know. And thank you, once again, for forgiving me."

Yet, in spite of their words, a sense of apprehension and unease still hung in the air like a foul odour. Peter thought about what Mark had said earlier. It wasn't easy . . . it wasn't easy at all. He marvelled at how emotions were such difficult things to deal with . . . they were so unlike physical wounds that could be covered with linen strips and herbs. They tended to fester in the dark recesses of one's being, only to surface every so often, and they would linger on in difficult silences . . . that was why Jesus taught them to work on forgiveness on a daily basis. The things hidden in darkness had to be brought

---

Wikipedia, s.v. "Paul the Apostle," https://en.wikipedia.org/wiki/Paul_the_Apostle#Physical_ appearance.

12. Paul took a long time to get over whatever happened between him and John Mark (Acts 13:13; 15:37–40). Only near the end of his life did he indicate that his perception of Mark had changed. See Colossians 4:10 and 2 Timothy 4:11.

into the light often, so that they might be exposed for what they were. He had noticed that all was not well between Mark and Paul. He wondered what had happened. Neither Barnabas nor Paul had spoken in Antioch about a problem with John Mark.

"Come," Mary urged, once more trying hard to ease the strain, "you must be tired."

"Tired and thirsty, yes," Barnabas said. "Thank you for your kind hospitality. You are such an example to all of us. I always pray we will meet someone like you in the cities we visit while on our trips."

"And, do you?"

"Most of the time . . . but still you tend to anticipate the needs of your guests like no one else."

"The community named you well, Barnabas . . . you are such an encourager."

"One who speaks truth in his encouragement, I hope?"

Mary laughed. In one sense, it was good to have a full house again. Things had been so quiet, too quiet, and Mark too broody and glum.

* * *

The heat in the room was rising. The lively and highly animated discussions between the apostles and the delegates from the two sides of the conflict added to the heightening sense of claustrophobia. One hundred and twenty had gathered in this room together at one time in the past, but that had been very different . . . they had been united in prayer . . . and they had all been Jewish believers. Paul and Barnabas and other delegates from Antioch were trying to make themselves heard above the din. They were still telling the assembly about what God had been doing in their ministry when a group of believers who belonged to the sect of the Pharisees stood up and shouted that Gentiles ought to submit to the requirements of the law of Moses before allowing them to become members of the faith community. This touched Paul deeply as they were men well known to him as he had once been a Pharisee himself. They seemed to be objecting to one man in particular who had come with them to Jerusalem.

"Now would be a good time to say something, Peter," Perpetua urged her husband.

Peter motioned with his hands that he wanted quiet. Out of respect for one esteemed as a pillar of the community, they fell silent.

"I need not remind you, brethren, as I am sure you all remember that not too long ago, God chose me to bring the gospel to the Gentiles in Caesarea. I was as surprised as you all were at the time, that God, who knows the heart of every individual,[13] poured out his Holy Spirit on them even before I had finished speaking." Peter paused for a moment and looked at each person in the room individually to see if there was any disagreement, but there was none. "God poured out his Holy Spirit on uncircumcised Gentiles, just as he had poured him out on us . . . thus making no distinction between them and us, purifying each heart through faith."

Peter looked over at Barnabas. He was beaming and his eyes were alight, as with fire. Smiling he urged Peter to continue with a nod.

"If this is the case, then why are you putting God to the test now? If God accepted the Caesarean Gentiles without reservation, who then are we to put extra burdens on the necks of the Gentiles . . . burdens, I hasten to add, that our own forefathers were not able to bear themselves? Far be it from us to do so, brethren! No! We believe that we have been granted salvation by the grace of our Lord Jesus . . . the same is true for the Gentiles."

At this point Peter looked over at Barnabas and Paul, indicating that it was time for them to build on what he had said. He sat down and Perpetua laid her hand gently on his and smiled. She did not need to speak . . . he knew her heart and he was encouraged.

Barnabas began by telling them what had happened in Antioch . . . how the community there was fully integrated in the faith without ethnic or linguistic division. Paul took over as he told them about the miraculous things God had done among the Gentiles through them as they travelled from place to place. No one said a word as everyone was in awe of the gracious mercy of God.

"Then from Attalia, we sailed back to Antioch, where we had been committed to this work by the grace of God. Once we arrived, we gathered our community together and reported to them all that the Lord had done through us and how he had opened wide the door of faith to the Gentiles."

Barnabas then spoke once again, bringing their contribution to a close, "It was while we were in Antioch that the question arose for which we are here seeking an answer today. We pray that we, as the one body of our Lord Jesus, might be led by the Spirit to put an end to further disagreements and deliberation among us."

They both sat down at this point. All eyes turned to James, the brother of Jesus. He was a godly man and well respected as a holy and devout man, even among the non-believing leaders[14] . . . they all sought his wise guidance.

"Well, brethren, we have all heard what Simon has said."

---

13. 1 Samuel 16:7; 1 Kings 8:39; Psalm 44:21.

14. Eusebius, *Ecclesiastical History* 2.23; Josephus, *Antiquities of the Jews*, 20.9.1.

Simon! Peter was at first surprised to hear him call him by his old, Hebrew name, but then he realized that this would carry more weight with the strict religious party.

"Simon has laid out before us the case that God has chosen for himself, followers from the Gentiles without reservation. This is in agreement with what the Scriptures say: 'In that day, I will rebuild the booth of David . . . I will repair its breaches and rebuild its ruins and build it as firm as it once was . . . so that the nations might seek after God, the Gentiles who bear my name, says the LORD who will bring all these things to pass.'"[15] He paused to allow those gathered to process what he had just quoted.

"For this reason, I believe we ought not to add any further requirements for conversion upon those whom God has clearly chosen to turn to him. We must not make it any more difficult for them as it already is." A low murmur of agreement hummed in the room.

"However," James raised his hand to indicate that he was not finished, "however, I do believe we ought to write to them to tell them to abstain from things that would be particularly repulsive to their Jewish brethren . . . namely, from eating food that has been offered to idols,[16] from all sexual deviancies,[17] and from eating any meat with its lifeblood in it, like that taken from strangled animals.[18] They know the law of Moses, as it has been read and expounded on in the synagogues in every city for a long time now."

"This would fulfil the command of our Lord to love our neighbour as we love ourselves," Peter said to Perpetua. "It is not compromise . . . it is love."

"If only we would always consider others before we say or do anything," she replied, "our world would be a better place."

"Yes . . . to always be humble and to esteem others better than ourselves . . . a difficult thing to do as we are all too quick to think of ourselves first, but one that would be worthy to pursue."

After further discussion and prayers for further guidance and affirmation, it was decided that a letter to this effect be written to the believers in Antioch, to be delivered by Judas and Silas as representatives of the community in Jerusalem. These men would accompany Barnabas and Paul to confirm the decision taken by the council through their own testimony.

---

15. Amos 9:11–12; Isaiah 45:21.

16. Exodus 34:15; Numbers 25:2; see also 1 Corinthians 8:1–13; Revelation 2:14, 20.

17. Leviticus 18:1–30; 20:10–21; Deuteronomy 22:22–29; 23:17; 27:20–23.

18. Leviticus 3:17; 7:26–27; 17:10–12; Deuteronomy 12:16.

As Paul was in a great hurry to take this message back to Antioch, the group left the following morning early. Barnabas insisted on taking John Mark with them.

Peter and Perpetua, on the other hand, chose to remain in Jerusalem. They had received word that Emperor Claudius had finally made good his threat to expel all Jews from Rome. Jude, Rachel, and Petronilla had already sailed for Caesarea. Peter felt he needed the rest. They would travel back to Rome once they were refreshed and spiritually restored.

* * *

18

Final Jerusalem Visit and Seasons of Change

Jude, how are you?" Peter asked. He had just arrived back in Jerusalem from Rome, having been summoned by the community there after the murder of James, the brother of Jesus.[1] Perpetua had chosen to remain in Rome with Petronilla to look after their precious family of orphans and destitute women. Mark had left them early to establish the church in Alexandria.

"We are still in shock," he replied, "we came for a visit . . . not a funeral."

"I still don't understand what happened . . . and why?"

"Well as you know, James regularly went to the temple. He prayed for them every day, his knees were calloused. And they all held him in high esteem . . . all of them . . . every sect, even the Essenes and you know how strict they are. But James was zealous for the law.[2] 'Faith without works is dead,'[3] he always said. But that was not enough for the Pharisees, apparently. They wanted him to convince the others that Jesus was not who he is. When he refused, they threw him down from the pinnacle of the temple . . . you know where the shofar blower always stands?"

"Yes, I know. How terrible."

"That's not the worst of it. The fall didn't kill him.[4] They tell me that as broken as his poor body was, he managed to push himself up onto his knees . . . those scabby, hardened knees . . . and then he began to pray for them! The Pharisees on the ground were horrified and they began to stone him. You see

---

1. Josephus, *Antiquities* 20.9.

2. Eusebius, *Ecclesiastical History*, 2.23.

3. James 2:17.

4. The following account is taken from Eusebius's *Ecclesiastical History*, 2.23 where he quotes from Hegesippus, a second-century believer.

they could do that because there was no Roman governor . . . they were a law to themselves. One of the priests, a son of the Rechabites, I believe, tried to stop them, but a fanatical launderer rushed at him and crushed his head with his launderer's club."

"Has the new procurator arrived yet?" Peter asked.

"Albinus? Yes. He has removed Ananus from his position as high priest . . . but the harm has been done."

"I take it that his action has stopped any further actions against our brethren?"

"Yes. There is a fragile peace . . . but it is fragile, Peter. Many of the brethren no longer feel safe here."

"I was just about to ask . . . how are they dealing with this?"

"Well, some have already fled to the other side of the Jordan, to Pella,[5] but for those who still live here . . . well, they deal with the unpredictability of the unbelieving Jews as best they can. Right now, they are hoping you will help them elect a new leader for the community here."

"Yes . . . yes, I expect they are. We must gather them together for prayer. There is no other way than to wait on the Holy Spirit for guidance in this matter."

"On another matter, Peter . . ."

"Yes?"

"I have written a letter to the communities we have served . . . a general letter . . . but I felt they needed to hear from us as soon as possible. There are some lapsed believers that are using the death of James as proof that Jesus will not return."

"Yes, we have heard this too . . . even before this awful event."

"I think it will be good for you to write to them as well . . . they see you as the pillar of the church. I am only the brother of James."

"You are our Lord's brother."

"Yes, but still. I think you and James . . . well, they look up to you and they will be in need of a word of guidance."

"These trouble-makers . . . the false teachers. What are they saying exactly? Do you know?"

"From what I've been told it sounds like the teaching of a Greek philosopher . . . a man by the name of Epicurus."

"I must admit, I am not well acquainted with his teaching."

"Well, he taught that God is completely removed from the lives of humans . . . that God is completely transcendent and aloof and therefore

---

5. Eusebius, *Ecclesiastical History* 3, 5.

uninvolved in our affairs. To him there is no divine plan . . . and no divine retribution. According to him, we ought to live as we please . . . to gratify ourselves as best we can, without overindulgence, mind you."

"And this is what the false teachers are advocating?"

"It seems like it, yes. This is why they question the prophetic word . . . they call them clever fictional fables. Only a God who cares for humanity will intervene on behalf of his people . . . and they don't like that teaching, so they scoff at the predictions of the destruction of Jerusalem. James's murder has added fuel to their argument."

"How so?"

"Well, it was Stephen first, then other brethren under the persecution of Paul. And then Herod killed James, John's brother, and now James, my brother. Our generation is passing away and the vestiges of Judaism . . . Jerusalem, the temple . . . in spite of what Jesus said, that not one stone would be left upon another . . . that all this would take place within the space of this generation . . . well, they are still standing. Nothing has changed, they say."[6]

"All that is reserved for the flames . . . you know that."[7]

"Yes, but they do not. They say that because these elements of the old order still remain as they always have, that there will be no judgement . . . that there is no coming of Jesus on the clouds."

"Like those in the times of Sodom and in the times of Noah . . . they scoffed as well."

"Yes, I said as much in my letter to them . . . and I reminded them that from the very beginning you warned us that in the last days there would be mockers. Wolves in sheep's clothing."

---

6. See Leithart's explanation regarding the reason for the letter being written in *The Promise of His Appearing*, 18.

7. For an excellent explanation of this interpretation of the word "elements" as the vestiges of the old covenant see John Owen's "Sermon X. Providential Changes, an Argument for Universal Holiness," https://www.ccel.org/ccel/owen/sermons.iv.xiii.html. See also Galatians 4:3, 9; Colossians 2:8, 20; Hebrews 5:12 where the same Greek word is used to denote the basic principles of the law. I believe Peter is speaking about the destruction of Jerusalem that took place in AD 70 where an out-of-control fire ravaged the city and the temple. I understand that the scoffers mentioned in 2 Peter were Jews or lapsed Christians. Both Jesus and the early Christians predicted the destruction of Jerusalem within that generation as proof that the Messiah had come and is now seated at the right hand of the Father in glory, but time had passed and with the death of yet another high level believer, they asked mockingly, "Where is he?" See also Hebrews 12:26–28. See also N. T. Wright, *Resurrection of the Son of God*, 463: "a linear movement of history, as in Judaism, moving forward towards judgment and new creation," and "the only way to the fulfilment of the creator's longing for a justice and goodness which will replace the present evil is for a process of fire, not simply to consume, but also to purge."

"You did well. Perhaps we could incorporate your letter into mine . . . that will show them that we are not divided, but that we are all of one mind. Many of them have received letters from Paul as well . . . we can mention him to add another witness to the truth."

"I have a copy of my letter here. We had several sent out to Asia and to Italy."

"Good, we can do the same with mine."

"Peter . . . this is such a terrible time . . . but I know that our God and Saviour is well able to keep all his children from falling . . . in spite of the threats of false teaching and of persecution, he will continue to work in us until he presents us without fault before his presence in glory. I truly believe that."

"Yes," Peter sighed, "we are in his hands . . . thankfully nothing can snatch us from his embrace. But we must be watchful, we must be vigilant, to use Mark's word, so that we will not be swept away by the error of those who are lawless. We must remind them of the truth so that they can be all the more eager to make their calling and election sure. I must make sure that my sermons – those that Mark recorded so long ago and then rewrote and copied for use in the communities – I must make sure that we provide more copies. They need to remember everything Jesus did and taught."

"We have well trained scribes at hand here."

"Good, let's get them started sooner rather than later. Then there is the matter of who must succeed your brother James. I believe many have gathered to discuss the matter. Am I correct?"

"Yes," Jude replied, "the favoured one appears to be Simeon, son of Clopas . . . you remember Clopas, Joseph's brother, don't you?"[8]

"I do. The Lord appeared to him on the road to Emmaus. My, that feels like a long time ago! His son is a good choice but let us see what the others say."

Peter was silent for a while, staring at his folded hands. He looked up at Jude and said softly, "Jude, there is something I need to share with you."

"Yes?"

"This may not be the best time to share this . . . you are still in mourning . . . but . . . I had a strange dream one night."

"A dream?"

"Yes . . . or at least I think it was a dream . . . a disturbing dream."[9]

---

8. Eusebius, *Ecclesiastical History* 3, 11.

9. I am using a story from the apocryphal Acts of Peter, more popularly known from the novel entitled *Quo Vadis: A Narrative of the Time of Nero*, written by the Polish author, Henryk Sienkiewicz.

"Please. Tell me."

"In my dream I was leaving Rome . . . or perhaps fleeing Rome. I was filled with a sense of foreboding, especially since I decided to leave Perpetua and Petronilla there this time . . . you know how busy they are with the orphaned children and the destitute."

"Yes?"

"Well, as I was leaving, I saw . . . and this is the disturbing part . . . I saw our Lord walking in the opposite direction."

"He was going to Rome?"

"Yes, I was leaving, but he was about to enter."

"Why?"

"Well that's what I was wondering too, so I asked him where he was going."

"And what did he say?"

"He said," suddenly Peter was overcome with emotion and he stifled a sob, "forgive me . . ."

"Not at all . . . here, drink some water."

"Thank you." Peter swallowed hard and then continued, "He said that he was going to Rome to be crucified again."

"How strange."

"Strange? Yes, I suppose so . . . but in my dream I understood what he meant. I was fleeing from my own death. I was trying to avoid martyrdom."

"Peter . . ."

"This is why I thought perhaps this was not the best time to tell you . . . but I really do believe that my passing is imminent."[10]

"I don't know what to say."

"I know. A strange dream . . . but it was so real, and I have been thinking about this all the while I was travelling. What if this is referring to what Jesus told me on the beach that day, you know that day when we had that life changing breakfast on the beach . . . he indicated that I would be crucified."

"Crucified? In Rome?"

"Well, he did not indicate a time or a place back then . . . but this dream."

"I would prevent you from leaving."

"As I would have prevented Jesus from going to the cross?"

"Was there trouble in Rome when you left?"

---

10. 2 Peter 1:13–15. Also, see Leithart's comparison of 2 Peter (δευτεραν επιοτολεν) with Deuteronomy (δευτερος νομος) in *Promise of His Appearing*, 19–20 (note 20).

"No, that's what made the dream all the more strange. I must admit I was tempted to run back to fetch Perpetua and Petronilla . . . but I don't think I would have been very convincing."

"Peter . . ."

"Thank you for your love, my brother . . . thank you for caring as you do . . . as you always have. But we have a letter to write."

"I will get the papyrus and the stylus . . . here is ink."

* * *

19

Winning the Race

The fire spread faster than anyone could have imagined. It began at night in the merchant shops close to the Palatine Hills, and, fanned on by the strong winds, it burned out of control for about six days. Then, after they thought it had been extinguished, it flared up again and burned for another three days. Two thirds of Rome now lay in ruins and many homes were reduced to little more than smoking ash heaps. Rumours spread thick and fast that it had been set by Emperor Nero himself . . . that he had hired men who pretended to be drunk who set the city alight. Others said no, Nero had been in Antium when the fire started. But the rumours intensified when he seemed to be all too keen to build a new palace for himself. Nero quickly diverted suspicion by placing the blame on the followers of Jesus.

At first, only a few of their members were arrested, but under the most agonizing torture they named others, until the entire Christian community was incriminated. The soldiers began to arrest as many as they could find and soon Nero began to display his gruesome vengeance publicly. Some he covered with the hides of wild animals to be torn apart by dogs, others he impaled, painted them with pitch, and then set them ablaze to provide light for his debauched garden parties.

"Oh Peter," Perpetua wept, "it is as if the devil himself walks among us . . . he and his diabolical hosts have risen from the abyss."

"Nero is just a man," Peter replied, "a wicked man and a powerful man, but a man . . . nothing more. He may encourage others to see him as a god, but he can exalt himself as much as he pleases. As John always says, he can multiply himself six hundred and sixty-six times, but he will never be the divine seven.[1]

---

1. Revelation 13:18.

But we know there is only one true God and he watches over us all . . . and will judge us all."

"Wouldn't now be a good time for Jesus to return, Papa?" Petronilla asked.

"Oh, my dearest daughter . . . for us, yes, but think of the masses of people who have never heard about him. We are so small in the scheme of things . . . there's a world out there filled with people who are still enslaved by Satan . . . people who are lost in the darkness of their miserable lives."

"But the tide is turning," Perpetua said, "the populace is repulsed by what Nero is doing . . . things may still change."

"That would be wonderful, my dear precious wife . . ." Peter began to say, but a sudden commotion outside stopped him from saying anything more. What happened next, happened so quickly that there were no words to be said. Soldiers burst into the room and grabbed them before they could react. Peter would remember the screams of his wife and daughter throughout their separation . . . which thankfully was short.

* * *

On the day they led him out to be crucified, he saw his beloved wife and daughter for the first time since they had been ripped apart. They had been wrapped in the skins of wild animals and were being led to the brink of a pit filled with starved dogs. Peter cried out to them to be strong and reminded them that they would soon be together again. They looked back with such peace-filled expressions, but before they could say anything in reply, they were cruelly thrown to the dogs.[2]

The crowds turned away in disgust. Many had had enough of Nero's bloodlust.

As they led him away, Peter remembered the words of Jesus as they strolled along the beach after that wonderful, life-changing breakfast. Jesus had spoken about the personal cost of following him. He had told Peter that a time would come when he, too, would be arrested and executed for his faith.

"The time has come, dear Lord," Peter prayed silently, "I have done what you commanded. I have made disciples for you and I trained them to do the same. I have multiplied myself, reproduced myself, and your followers are increasing. Just as you commanded, we have done what you did in your earthly ministry . . . and have done more . . . your words have gone out into all the earth."

---

2. See Clement of Alexandria, *Stromateis*, 7, 63:3; Eusebius, *Ecclesiastical History* 3, 30.2.

They laid him head down on the upside-down cross, as he had requested. A soldier knelt beside him with huge nails and a hammer in his hands.

"My father," he said quietly, looking down at Peter's hands, "forgive me . . . I have no choice."

At first Peter was so taken aback, he didn't know what to say.

"Many do not approve of what the emperor is doing. So many of us have secretly become believers in your God. We have never witnessed any faith like yours. You cheerfully go to your death . . . and we know it is because you believe that you have a life beyond this unhappy one."

"You believe in Jesus?" Peter said softly, trying not to attract undue attention to the soldier.

"I do . . . I have in my possession some of your writings. I took them before they were put to the torch. Forgive me."

"Read them . . . tell others," Peter whispered back. "Tell them to never stop telling others."

He felt a tear fall on his bare arm.

"Now do what you must do . . . quickly. I will see you again in the kingdom one day."

"Forgive me," the soldier said again.

"You are forgiven . . . and loved."

An unimaginable pain shot through his wrist and trailed down his arm with lightning speed as the nail crushed through bone and flesh. Then the other arm and his feet and legs. The jolt as the cross slipped into place, made the blood rush to his head. But in his spirit, he heard the words of Jesus, "Well done, good and faithful servant . . . enter into your well-earned rest."[3]

* * *

---

3. Eusebius, *Ecclesiastical History* 3, 1:2. For an interesting alternative theory regarding Peter's martyrdom by burning, see Timothy D. Barnes, "Another Shall Gird Thee: Probative Evidence for the Death of Peter," in Bond and Hurtado, *Peter in Early Christianity*, 76–95.

Appendixes

Appendixes

Appendix A

Presuppositions

General

- All Jewish boys (some say girls as well) knew the Torah and the Psalms by heart by age 10–13.
- All Jewish boys came of age at thirteen when they would start their apprenticeship, usually with their fathers, following family traditions and vocations.
- All Jewish boys were able to read and memorize Hebrew.
- All Jewish boys were fluent in Aramaic.
- All Jewish boys were conversant in Greek and Latin, especially in Galilee.
- All Jewish boys were aware of the general oral law, although they may not have known the finer details of it (cf. John 7:49).
- Gifted Jewish boys were given the opportunity to study further, as Saul/Paul under Gamaliel.

Jesus

- His mother, Mary, had the ability to string together passages of Scripture from memory.
- He astounded the law experts by age twelve.
- He was able to quote and allude to passages from the Torah, the Prophets, and the Writings.

Disciples

- As Galilean tradesmen, they would have been fluent in Aramaic, and conversant in Greek and Latin.
- They would have known at least the Torah and the Psalms by heart.

- They received intensive training from Jesus for a period of three to four years.
- They were able to comprehend Jesus's post-resurrection Bible studies that dealt with all the Scriptures.
- Post-Pentecost, they had unhindered access to the same three resources as Jesus, the Scriptures, direct access to the Father through prayer, and the power, wisdom, guidance, and leading of the Holy Spirit.
- Their knowledge astounded the law experts, especially since they were assumed to be "unschooled."
- They were together in Jerusalem for a period of eight to ten years post ascension.
- Saul met the disciples and stayed with them in Jerusalem for fifteen days.

Appendix B

Assumptions

- The disciples had committed most if not all of Scripture to memory. I have personally witnessed this type of memorization in oral communities and have heard of persecuted individuals in communities where the Bible has been outlawed memorizing whole books.
- They understood and interpreted the Scriptures according to Jesus's hermeneutic and by the illumination given by the Holy Spirit who brought to remembrance all Jesus had taught them and continually led them in all truth.
- They taught their converts as Jesus had taught them.
- Out-of-country Pentecost converts returned to the homes and thus needed instruction, making Epistles and Gospels necessary.
- Travel was made easier by good Roman roads and safer by the Pax Romana. There is no reason to think that the disciples did not travel extensively outside of the borders of Israel.
- Scribes were used which accounts for good Greek and differences in style between Epistles.
- They discussed and developed theology – I give the disciples a lot more credit than most modern scholars I have read – I do believe they understood more than some may think – at least Elizabeth and Thomas clearly believed Jesus to be divine.
- They composed Christian hymnody, liturgy, prayers, blessings, doxologies, and benedictions.
- They believed Jerusalem to be apostate and that the vestiges of the old covenant, the temple and the city of Jerusalem, would soon be destroyed as per Jesus's prophetic word, proving that the Son of Man was indeed seated in judgement at the right hand of the Father. According to Jesus, this would all take place within that particular generation, namely within a forty-year period, hence their repeated reminders that the Lord's word would be fulfilled in their own time.

- They believed Jerusalem to be the new Babylon according to Jesus's use of Old Testament images in his prophetic utterances.
- They believed themselves to be the new Jerusalem, the new Israel of God, the new non-geographical temple built with living stones, Jesus being the cornerstone and the apostles the foundation.
- As no mention is made of the destruction of Jerusalem as a past event in any of the New Testament writings, all books were written before AD 70.

Appendix C

Thesis, Tradition, and Timeline

A note on chronology and tradition. It is tricky to work out exactly what happened when and where in the life of Peter from Acts 9 through 12, and his life post Jerusalem Council, given the comments of Paul in Galatians 1:16–17 and 2 Corinthians 11:32–33, and two traditions regarding Peter's establishment of the churches in Antioch (AD 34)[1] and in Rome (AD 42). In his *Ecclesiastical History*, Eusebius also indicated that Peter visited churches in Cappadocia, Galatia, Pontus, and Bithynia.[2] I have tried to knit these together in the narrative.

I have Peter visit and organize the church in Antioch shortly after Saul/ Paul's conversion. After three years in Arabia, Saul/Paul returns to Damascus, but flees shortly afterwards to Jerusalem where he meets with Peter (AD 37). Because of threats he flees again, this time to Tarsus. Peter continues his mission in country and is present when the first Gentiles are brought into the church for which he gives a defence.

According to tradition he then goes to Rome in AD 42.[3] This might explain why Barnabas is chosen to go to Antioch to investigate the rumours of Gentile inclusion in the church in Antioch and not Peter.

As Acts has Peter imprisoned by Herod Agrippa in Jerusalem, I have him revisit all the churches in Asia as well as Antioch on his first return journey. On this return journey, he finds that Barnabas has brought Paul to Antioch and they have been there for some time. Once back in Jerusalem, he writes his first letter to the churches in northern modern-day Turkey and continues to work on Mark's record of his sermons together with Silas. With regard to the writing of the first epistle of Peter, I had three choices. The first option was to have Peter write this epistle during his first return visit to Jerusalem

---

1. Eusebius, *Ecclesiastical History* 3, 36. See also Origen's homilies on Luke VI, 4. Patrologia Graeca 13:1814, Wikipedia, s.v. "Saint Peter," https://en.wikipedia.org/wiki/Saint_Peter.

2. Eusebius, *Ecclesiastical History* 3, 1:2.

3. Article is available here: https://biblicalstudies.org.uk/peter.php.

from Rome, prior to the decision of the Jerusalem Council. The second option would have been the period immediately before or after the Jerusalem Council. As there is no mention in his first epistle of any decision with regard to this council and its decision, I preferred the first option. Silas and John Mark would have been present in Jerusalem for both first and second options. The third option would have been to go with a later date. A later date has been preferred by some scholars mainly because they assume that Peter is familiar with the letters of Paul, and that Babylon is a metaphor for Rome. As far as the identity of this Babylon, please see footnote 10 on p124. I do not find their arguments compelling and so have chosen to go with an early date.[4]

While Peter is still in Jerusalem, Barnabas and Saul/Paul bring relief aid to the community in Judea. James, Peter's former fishing partner, is beheaded by Agrippa and Peter narrowly escapes execution and flees back to Rome. I have him return the same way he came, visiting the churches along the way. Barnabas and Saul/Paul return to Antioch taking John Mark with them.

On his second return journey from Rome, I have Peter follow his usual route, including a visit to the church in Antioch. This visit gives rise to the unpleasantness mentioned by Paul in Galatians and leads to the Jerusalem Council. This is after John Mark's return to Jerusalem during the first missionary journey of Barnabas and Saul/Paul.

Post Jerusalem Council, Peter returns to Rome in AD 50 after a stay in Jerusalem, as Claudius had expelled all Jews from the imperial city in AD 49. Mark goes to Cyprus with Barnabas and then, according to tradition, on to Alexandria where he establishes the church there in AD 49.

James, the Lord's brother, is executed by the Jewish high priest in AD 62.[5] Hegesippus, a second-century theologian, wrote that, following James's death, Jesus's cousin Simeon, was chosen to be leader of the Jerusalem church in his stead.[6] It is possible that Peter was present in Jerusalem for this deliberation and that he wrote his second epistle at that time. In the light of this tragic event and the fact that the bastion of Judaism, Jerusalem and the temple (the very

---

4. Clement appears to be quoting from 1 Peter 4:8 and 5:5 in 1 Clement 49:5 and 30:2 respectively, perhaps indicating an early date for 1 Peter.

5. See Wikipedia, s.v. "James, Brother of Jesus," https://en.wikipedia.org/wiki/James,_brother_of_Jesus.

6. See David Hulme, "James, Brother of Jesus," *Vision*, The Apostles, Part 12, https://www.vision.org/the-apostle-james-the-brother-of-jesus-868, and Philip Schaff, "Chapter XXIII.— The Martyrdom of James, Who Was Called the Brother of the Lord," *Nicene and Post-Nicene Fathers, Series 2, Volume 1*, online Christian Classics Ethereal Library, https://www.ccel.org/ccel/schaff/npnf201.iii.vii.xxiv.html.

source of their ongoing persecution), had not been destroyed yet as prophesied by Jesus and the apostles, some lapsed Christian Jews seem to have begun to question the prediction of Jesus's return. I believe this is the primary reason Peter wrote his second epistle to the churches he had served in Asia and in Rome.[7] If John A. T. Robinson is correct in his assumptions with regard to the similarities between the writings of Jude and 2 Peter, then it is possible that Jude (who could very well have travelled with Peter to Rome and elsewhere seeing that he is mentioned together with Peter in 1 Corinthians) wrote his short epistle to the Christians of Asia and Rome in Peter's absence, and then served as scribe for Peter's second epistle addressed to the same community.[8] Given the fact that the subject matter of first and second Peter appear to be different, I believe the reference in 2 Peter regarding a previous letter refers not to 1 Peter, but to chapters 1 and 2 of 2 Peter. Scribes could very well have joined the two at a later stage as some have argued is the case with parts of 1 and 2 Corinthians.

Fire engulfed and destroyed much of Rome in AD 64, which Nero blamed on the Christians. Peter was probably executed in the summer of AD 65,[9] being crucified upside down by request according to tradition.[10]

Timeline

Crucifixion, resurrection, ascension, Pentecost	AD 33[11]
Jewish converts from different nations return home	AD 33
Jerusalem, Judea, and Samaria. Stephen martyred, Philip's ministry	AD 33–34
Saul Converted	AD 34 – Arabia three years

---

7. For a good defense for the Petrine authorship, see Larry R. Helyer, *The Life and Witness of Peter* (Downers Grove, IL: IVP Academic, 2012), 205–71.

8. Robinson, *Redating the New Testament*, 193–94.

9. Tacitus in his Annals 15:38–41, seems to indicate that the persecution of Christians only started after the rebuilding program in Rome had been underway for a time. Also, the use of burning impaled Christians as lamps for Nero's garden parties indicates either the late Spring or early summer of AD 65.

10. For an insightful summary of Peter's life, see "St. Peter, Prince of the Apostles," *New Advent*, https://www.newadvent.org/cathen/11744a.htm.

11. For dating the crucifixion, "Dating the Crucifixion," *The Star of Bethlehem*, https://www.bethlehemstar.com/the-day-of-the-cross/dating-the-crucifixion/ and "Pilate and Sejanus," *The Star of Bethlehem*, https://www.bethlehemstar.com/the-day-of-the-cross/pilate-and-sejanus/.

Peter establishes the church in Antioch	AD 34 (tradition)
Saul returns to Damascus and escapes to Jerusalem	AD 37
Herod Agrippa I appointed king	AD 37
Saul with Peter	AD 37
Saul to Tarsus	AD 37
Peter heals Aeneas and Dorcas and brings the gospel to Cornelius	AD 38
Peter travels to Caesarea, Antioch, Pontus, Galatia, Cappadocia, Asia, and Bithynia on to Rome	AD 39–42 (tradition)
Herod Agrippa I receives Judea and Samaria	AD 41
Barnabas goes to Antioch	AD 42/43
Peter returns to Jerusalem via Pontus, Bithynia, Galatia, Cappadocia, and Antioch	AD 44
The writing of 1 Peter	AD 44
Barnabas and Saul in Jerusalem with gifts of food from Antioch	AD 44
Execution of James the brother of John, departure of twelve to international missions	AD 44
Imprisonment and escape of Peter (to Caesarea, Antioch, Pontus, Galatia, Cappadocia, Asia, and Bithynia to Rome)	AD 44
Death of Herod Agrippa	AD 44
Barnabas, Paul, and Mark to Antioch and then on their first missionary journey	AD 44–48
Peter back to Jerusalem via Pontus, Bithynia, Galatia, Cappadocia, Asia, and Antioch	AD 48
Peter and Paul's clash in Antioch	AD 48
Jerusalem Council	AD 49
Jews expelled from Rome	AD 49
Mark to Cyprus, perhaps on to Rome in AD 50 to join Peter and then later to Alexandria where he founded the church there	AD 49 (biblical and tradition)
Peter returns to Rome	AD 50
Nero becomes Emperor	AD 54
James, the brother of Jesus executed	AD 62
The writing of 2 Peter	AD 62
Fire in Rome	AD 64
Peter returns to Rome and is executed	AD 65

Bibliography

Adeyemo, Tokunboh, ed. *Africa Bible Commentary: A One-Volume Commentary Written by 70 African Scholars*. Nairobi: WordAlive, 2006.

Bartlett, David L. *The First Letter of Peter*. In *The New Interpreters Bible*, vol. 12. Nashville: Abingdon, 1998.

Bockmuehl, Markus. *Simon Peter in Scripture and Memory: The New Testament Apostle in the Early Church*. Grand Rapids, MI: Baker, 2012.

Bond, Helen K., and Larry Hurtado, eds. *Peter in Early Christianity*. Grand Rapids, MI: Eerdmans, 2015.

Brown, Raymond E., Karl P. Donfried, and John Reumann, eds. *Peter in the New Testament: A Collaborative Assessment by Protestant and Roman Catholic Scholars*. Eugene, OR: Wipf & Stock, 1973.

Clark, George W. *Harmony of the Acts of the Apostles*. Philadelphia: American Baptist Publication Society, 1897.

Clarke, W. K. Lowther. *The First Epistle of Clement to the Corinthians*. London: SPCK, 1937.

The Complete Apocrypha. Columbia: Covenant Press, 2018.

Cullmann, Oscar. *Peter: Disciple, Apostle, Martyr*. New York: Meridan Books, 1958.

Day, John. *Temple and Worship in Biblical Israel*. London: T&T Clark, 2007.

Eastman, David L. *The Ancient Martyrdom Accounts of Peter and Paul*. Atlanta: SBL Press, 2015.

Ehrman, Bart D. *After the New Testament: A Reader in Early Christianity*. Oxford: Oxford University Press, 1999.

———. *Peter, Paul, and Mary Magdalene: The Followers of Jesus in History and Legend*. Oxford: Oxford University Press, 2006.

Elliot, John H. *1 Peter: A New Translation with Introduction and Commentary*. New York: Doubleday, 2000.

Ellsworth, Roger. *Simon Peter: Encountering the Preacher at Pentecost*. Leominster: Day One Publications, 2007.

Gonzalez, Catherine Gunsalus. *1 & 2 Peter and Jude*. Louisville: Westminster John Knox, 2010.

Goppelt, Leonhard. *A Commentary on 1 Peter*. Grand Rapids, MI: Eerdmans, 1993.

Grabbe, Lester L. *An Introduction to Second Temple Judaism: History and Religion of the Jews in the Time of Nehemiah, the Maccabees, Hillel and Jesus*. London: T&T Clark, 2010.

Grant, Michael. *Saint Peter: A Biography*. New York: Scribner, 1994.

Hart, J. H. A. *The First Epistle General of Peter*. In *The Expositor's Greek Testament*, vol. 5. Peabody, MA: Hendrickson, 2002.

Helyer, Larry R. *The Life and Witness of Peter*. Downers Grove, IL: IVP Academic, 2012.

Hengel, Martin. *Saint Peter: The Underestimated Apostle*. Grand Rapids, MI: Eerdmans, 2010.

Immanuel, Babu. *Acts of the Apostles: An Exegetical and Contextual Commentary, India Commentary on the New Testament*. Minneapolis: Fortress, 2017.

Josephus, Flavius. *The Complete Works of Josephus*. Grand Rapids, MI: Kregel, 1981.

Knowling, R. J. *The Acts of the Apostles*. Peabody, MA: Hendrickson, 2002.

Kurz, William S. *Acts of the Apostles: Catholic Commentary on Sacred Scripture*. Grand Rapids, MI: Baker Academic, 2013.

Lane, William L. *The Gospel According to Mark*. Grand Rapids, MI: Eerdmans, 1974.

Leithart, Peter. *The Promise of His Appearing: An Exposition of Second Peter*. Moscow: Canon, 2004.

———. *Revelation 1–11*. International Theological Commentary. London: T&T Clark, 2018.

———. *Revelation 12–22*. International Theological Commentary. London: T&T Clark, 2018.

Maier, Paul L. *Eusebius: The Church History: A New Translation with Commentary*. Grand Rapids, MI: Kregel, 1999.

Martin, Francis, ed. *Acts*. Downers Grove, IL: InterVarsity Press, 2006.

Marxsen, Willi. *Der Evangelist Markus: Studien zur Redaktionsgeschichte des Evangeliums*. Gottingen: Vanderhoeck & Ruprecht, 1959.

Meyendorff, John, ed. *The Primacy of Peter*. New York: St Vladimir's Seminary Press, 1992.

Moss, Candida. "Fashioning Mark: Early Christian Discussions about the Scribe and Status of the Second Gospel." *New Testament Studies* 67, no. 2 (2021): 181–204.

Park, Sejin, *Pentecost and Sinai: The Festival of Weeks as a Celebration of the Sinai Event*. New York: T&T Clark, 2008.

Parsons, Mikeal C. *Acts*. Grand Rapids, MI: Baker Academic, 2008.

Pelikan, Jaroslav. *Acts*. Grand Rapids, MI: Brazos Press, 2005.

Pennington, M. Basil. *In Peter's Footsteps: Learning to be a Disciple*. New York: Doubleday, 1985.

Perkins, Pheme. *Peter: Apostle for the Whole Church*. Minneapolis: Fortress, 2000.

Pinter, Dean. *Acts*. The Story of God Bible Commentary. Grand Rapids, MI: Zondervan, 2019.

Quast, Kevin. *Peter and the Beloved Disciple: Figures for a Community in Crisis*. Sheffield: Sheffield Academic Press, 1989.

Ray, Stephen K. *Upon this Rock: St. Peter and the Primacy of Rome in Scripture and the Early Church*. San Francisco: Ignatius Press, 1999.

Roberts, Alexander, and James Donaldson, eds. *The Ante-Nicene Fathers: Translations of the Writings of the Fathers down to A.D. 325*. Grand Rapids, MI: Eerdmans, 1989.

Robinson, John A. T. *Redating the New Testament*. London: SCM, 1976.

Schnabel, Eckhard J. *Acts: Exegetical Commentary on the New Testament*. Grand Rapids, MI: Zondervan, 2012.

Schoedel, William R. *Ignatius of Antioch: A Commentary on the Letters of Ignatius of Antioch*. Philadelphia: Fortress, 1985.

Schreiner, Thomas R. *Galatians: Exegetical Commentary on the New Testament*. Grand Rapids, MI: Zondervan, 2010.

Senior, Donald P., and Daniel J. Harrington. *1 Peter, Jude, and 2 Peter*. Collegeville, MN: Liturgical Press, 2003.

Spencer, F. Scott. *Journeying through Acts: A Literary-Cultural Reading*. Peabody, MA: Hendrickson, 2004.

Sproul, R. C. *1–2 Peter*. Wheaton, IL: Crossway, 2011.

Strachan, R. H. *The Second Epistle General of Peter*. The Expositor's Greek Testament. Peabody, MA: Hendrickson, 2002.

Thiede, Carsten P. *Simon Peter: From Galilee to Rome*. Grand Rapids, MI: Zondervan, 1988.

Valdez, Erbey Galvan. *On the Shores of Perga: How John Mark's Departure from the First Pauline Missionary Journey Changed the Gentile World*. Indiana: Westbow Press, 2020.

Vang, Preben, and Terry Carter. *Telling God's Story: The Biblical Narrative from Beginning to End*. Nashville: Broadman & Holman, 2006.

Vanhoye, Albert, and Peter S. Williamson. *Galatians: Catholic Commentary on Sacred Scriptures*. Grand Rapids, MI: Baker Academic, 2019.

Watson, Duane F. *The Second Letter of Peter*. In *The New Interpreters Bible*, vol. 12. Nashville: Abingdon, 1998.

Watson, Duane F., and Terrance Callan. *First and Second Peter*. Grand Rapids, MI: Baker Academic, 2012.

Wigram, George V. *The Analytical Greek Lexicon of the New Testament*. Peabody, MA: Hendrickson, 1983.

Wright, Christopher J. H. *Knowing the Holy Spirit Through the Old Testament*. Downers Grove, IL: IVP Academic, 2006.

Wright, N. T. *Jesus and the Victory of God*. Minneapolis: Fortress, 1996.

———. *The Resurrection and the Son of God*. London: SPCK, 2003.

Bibles Consulted

Africa Study Bible. Edited by John Jusu. Oasis International, 2016.

The Greek New Testament, 3rd edition. Edited by Kurt Aland, Matthew Black, Carlo M. Martini, Bruce M. Metzger, and Allen Wikgren. Stuttgart: United Bible Societies, 1983.

The Interlinear Bible. Edited by Jay P. Green, Sr. Grand Rapids, MI: Baker Books, 1985.

The Jerusalem Bible: Reader's Edition. New York: Doubleday & Company, 1968.

JPS Hebrew-English Tanakh: The Traditional Hebrew Text and the New JPS Translation, 2nd edition. Philadelphia: The Jewish Publication Society, 2000.

New Living Translation. Carol Stream, IL: Tyndale House Publishers, 2015.

NIV Archaeological Study Bible. Grand Rapids, MI: Zondervan, 2005.

NRSV Cultural Backgrounds Study Bible: Bringing to Life the Ancient World of Scripture. Edited by Keener Walton. Grand Rapids, MI: Zondervan, 2019.

The Passion Translation. Edited by Brian Simmons. BroadStreet Publishing Group, 2018.

A Reader's Hebrew and Greek Bible. Edited by Richard J. Goodrich, Albert Lukaszewski, Philip A. Brown, and Bryan W. Smith. Grand Rapids, MI: Zondervan, 2008.

Langham
PARTNERSHIP

Langham Literature and its imprints are a ministry of Langham Partnership.

Langham Partnership is a global fellowship working in pursuit of the vision God entrusted to its founder John Stott –

> *to facilitate the growth of the church in maturity and Christ-likeness through raising the standards of biblical preaching and teaching.*

Our vision is to see churches in the Majority World equipped for mission and growing to maturity in Christ through the ministry of pastors and leaders who believe, teach and live by the word of God.

Our mission is to strengthen the ministry of the word of God through:
- nurturing national movements for biblical preaching
- fostering the creation and distribution of evangelical literature
- enhancing evangelical theological education

especially in countries where churches are under-resourced.

Our ministry

Langham Preaching partners with national leaders to nurture indigenous biblical preaching movements for pastors and lay preachers all around the world. With the support of a team of trainers from many countries, a multi-level programme of seminars provides practical training, and is followed by a programme for training local facilitators. Local preachers' groups and national and regional networks ensure continuity and ongoing development, seeking to build vigorous movements committed to Bible exposition.

Langham Literature provides Majority World preachers, scholars and seminary libraries with evangelical books and electronic resources through publishing and distribution, grants and discounts. The programme also fosters the creation of indigenous evangelical books in many languages, through writer's grants, strengthening local evangelical publishing houses, and investment in major regional literature projects, such as one volume Bible commentaries like *The Africa Bible Commentary* and *The South Asia Bible Commentary*.

Langham Scholars provides financial support for evangelical doctoral students from the Majority World so that, when they return home, they may train pastors and other Christian leaders with sound, biblical and theological teaching. This programme equips those who equip others. Langham Scholars also works in partnership with Majority World seminaries in strengthening evangelical theological education. A growing number of Langham Scholars study in high quality doctoral programmes in the Majority World itself. As well as teaching the next generation of pastors, graduated Langham Scholars exercise significant influence through their writing and leadership.

To learn more about Langham Partnership and the work we do visit **langham.org**